The Address Book
of Children's Authors
and Illustrators

Chosen and presented by Gervase Phinn

The Address Book of Children's Authors and Illustrators
LL01325
© Gervase Phinn
ISBN 1 85503 355 0
All rights reserved
First published 2002
Reprinted 2002
The right of Gervase Phinn to be identified as the author of this work has been asserted by him in accordance with sections 77 and 78 of the Copyright, Designs and Patents Act 1988

Printed in the UK for LDA

LDA, Duke Street, Wisbech, Cambs PE13 2AE UK
3195 Wilson Drive NW, Grand Rapids, MI 49544 USA

Note: Use of the term 'authors' within the text denotes both authors and illustrators.

ontents

Preface

Treasure

Opening the covers of a book
Is like lifting the lid of a treasure chest.
Look inside and you will find
Golden stories and glittering characters.

Some are given a map to show them where X marks the spot,
Some are given the precious key to open up the lock,
Some are helped to lift the heavy lid,
But for some it will remain a buried treasure.

Gervase Phinn

Introduction

What are needed are texts that fascinate children and convince them that reading is delightful and helps one to gain a better understanding of oneself and others – in short, of the world we live in and how to live in it. To achieve this, texts should stimulate and enrich a child's imagination, as fairy tales do, and should develop the child's literary sensitivities, as good poems are apt to do. The texts should also present the child with literary images of the world, of nature and of man, as these have been created by great writers.

From B. Bettelheim and K. Zelan (1991). *On Learning to Read*, Penguin

As a child I well recall the first reading scheme book which I trawled through. It was called *The Radiant Way* and the front cover depicted two very happy children – the small girl gambolling gaily over a grassy knoll covered in daisies, a posy clutched in her hand; and the little boy, in sparklingly clean shirt, checked shorts and white ankle socks, skipping ahead merrily. Two smiling rabbits looked on. Then came the text:

Come. Mother, come.
Pat has a cod.
Ann ran for Mother.
See, Mother, Pat has a cod.
Bring the pot, Ann, for the cod.
Thank you, Ann, for the pot.
Bring the cod, Pat, to the pot.
Thank you, Pat, for the cod.

There was no author or illustrator mentioned on the cover. I, the son of a steel worker in Rotherham, had little in common with the pristine children and their innocent antics in *The Radiant Way*. This comment on *The Radiant Way* is no criticism of its authors or its publisher; it was typical of a number of reading schemes offered at the time. At home the book was put aside and my mother would turn to "real" stories and poems by challenging and illuminating authors. She would tell and read folk and fairy tales, cautionary fables, memoirs and myths, legends and adventures. She introduced me to Beatrix Potter, Hans Christian Andersen and Lewis Carroll; to Tolstoy's wondrous fables, *Babar the King*, the parables of Jesus, *The Flowers of St Francis*, *The Wind in the Willows*, *The Velveteen Rabbit* and *The Wizard of Oz* – to stories, poems and pictures that fascinated and delighted me and that will continue to fascinate and delight children for generations to come.

I was a fortunate child. To use the phrase of my favourite poet, R.S. Thomas, I "swam in a pool of language". I sat each night on my mother's knee, read to her, told her stories, talked about books, was taken to the library and the bookshop, and was bought books at Christmas and for my birthdays and helped to build up a little library of my own in my bedroom. I was raised in a richly motivating reading environment where books were important and valued, the environment that produces the lifelong reader.

It has, of course, been ever thus. The poet Coleridge wrote of his childhood:

> I read every book that came my way without distinction – and my father was very fond of me, and used to take me on his knee, and hold long conversations with me. I remember, that at eight years old, I walked with him one winter evening from a farmer's house, a mile from Ottery – and he told me the names of the stars – and how Jupiter was a thousand times larger than our world and that the other twinkling stars were suns that had worlds rolling around them – and when I came home, he shewed me how they rolled round. I heard him with profound delight and admiration; but without the least mixture of wonder or incredulity. For from my early reading of Faery Tales, and Genii etc. etc. – my mind had been habituated to the Vast.

From R. Holmes (1990). *Coleridge: Early Visions*
(quoted: from Coleridge's *Letters 1, 1780*), Hodder & Stoughton

This is what parents, teachers, librarians, booksellers and authors should be about – habituating children to the vastness of literature. If we provide children with a variety of exciting and challenging texts – with stories, poems and illustrations that fascinate, excite, intrigue and amuse; that give them fresh insights, that open their minds and imaginations and that introduce them to the wonderful richness and range of language and art – then we produce avid, enthusiastic and discriminatory readers and offer them the very best models for their own writing. This is no new philosophy. It has been a fundamental belief of all those who have attempted to open the wonderful world of literature, language and art to the young. The philosopher John Locke wrote over 300 years ago in *Some Thoughts Concerning Education*:

> When he can talk 'tis time he should begin to learn to read, but as to this, give me leave here to inculcate again what is very apt to be forgotten, namely that great care is to be taken that it be never made as a business to him nor he look upon it as a task. Their being forced and tied down to their books in an age at enmity with all such restraint, has I doubt not been reason why a great many have hated books and learning all their lives after. It is like a surfeit which leaves an aversion to learning not to be removed. Thus much for learning to read, which let him never be driven to nor chid for: cheat him into it if you can, but make it not a business for him. 'Tis better it be a year later before he can read than that he should this way get an aversion to learning. Use your skill to make his will supple and plaint to reason. Teach him to love credit and commendation, to abhor being thought ill or meanly of, especially by you and his mother, and then the rest will come all easily. When by these easy ways he begins to read, some easy pleasant book suited to his capacity should be put into

his hands wherein the entertainment might draw him on and reward his pains in reading.

Teachers know that to become avid and successful readers, their pupils need to be exposed to rich and stimulating material which will arouse their interest in and develop a love of reading. Children deserve to hear and read language and see illustrations of the very best, material which will make them smile and laugh, become captivated and curious, sometimes feel sad and a little scared and which will encourage them to want more and more and more. These principles are at the heart of the National Curriculum and the National Literacy Strategy Framework, both of which stress the vital importance of providing good-quality texts. All pupils are entitled to hear, read and discuss picture books, nursery rhymes, rhythmic verse, folk tales, legends, myths and other stories in different genre; to be exposed to literature and illustrations which will challenge and excite them; and to learn, through lively discussion and sensitive analysis of the texts, just how language works.

When I was elevated to the position of "free reader" at infant school and allowed to select my own reading material, I moved on to "real books" and devoured them. I was soon reading my way through the books on the library shelves: *The Coral Island, Black Beauty, The Children of the New Forest, The Black Arrow, Kidnapped, Lorna Doone, The Three Musketeers, The Man in the Iron Mask, Ivanhoe, The Black Tulip, Moby Dick, Moonfleet, Treasure Island, The Last of the Mohicans*. I would often stare at the name on the front of my reading book and wonder just what sort of person the writer was. What did Alexandre Dumas look like? Was R.D. Blackmore a man or a woman? Did Anna Sewell live in the country with stables full of horses? Where did Captain Marryat live? What was R.L. Stevenson's favourite book? Where did Sir Walter Scott get his ideas?

The Address Book of Children's Authors and Illustrators is a resource for teachers, librarians, parents and children, conceived out of a desire to introduce to you the very best and most popular children's authors and illustrators and get them to reveal to their avid readers something about themselves. In the fascinating autobiographies that fill the following pages, the authors reveal things about themselves that we might never have suspected or imagined and they have done so in a manner which I hope will inspire and encourage children to create their own stories, poems and illustrations.

Over 7,000 new children's books are published every year. Sadly, I have had to leave out some of my favourite authors and illustrators and probably some of yours too. Readers may be disappointed to find that a number of very popular and well-loved authors and illustrators are missing. Despite my best efforts, several did not wish to be included and I have, of course, respected this decision.

The authors and illustrators represented in *The Address Book* do not patronise their young readers. They know that children are curious, eager and sharply observant, and that they love stories, verse and pictures that absorb their attention and make demands upon them. They know that stories, poems and illustrations are massively important in developing children's language and imagination but they also recognise their significance in developing children's emotional literacy. Through their writing and their art the authors explore ideas of right and wrong, jealousy, friendship, disappointment, fear and happiness, being accepted and rejected, moral dilemmas and the making of choices in which the characters ultimately find security, comfort and love. They go to the very heart of children's joys and anxieties.

The appendices to this book are not an afterthought but a vital resource. They contain ideas, suggestions, lists, addresses and web sites which will be of help and interest to teachers and librarians who want to give children a full experience of books and their authors.

Let me conclude with the words of the Children's Poet Laureate. Anne Fine, writing in the *Guardian*, describes perfectly what a good book does for the reader:

> A book that lasts has to create a world so real that you can run your fingertips over its walls, feel its morning frostbite at your throat, and remember the people who lived there for a lifetime.

List of Children's Authors and Illustrators Included in The Address Book

Joan Aiken
Jez Alborough
Nicholas Allan
David Almond
Bernard Ashley

Nina Bawden
Ian Beck
Malorie Blackman
Tony Bradman
Ruth Brown
Anthony Browne
Alex Brychta

Eric Carle
Humphrey Carpenter
Dick Cate
Babette Cole
Helen Cooper
Susan Cooper
Wendy Cope
Pie Corbett
Helen Cowcher
Helen Craig
Helen Cresswell
Gillian Cross
Kevin Crossley-Holland

Colin Dann
Peter Dixon
Berlie Doherty

Anne Fine
Catherine Fisher
Pauline Fisk
John Foster

Jane Gardam
Alan Garner
Paul Geraghty
Adèle Geras
Debi Gliori
Pippa Goodhart
Mick Gowar

Michael Hardcastle
Michael Harrison
Anne Harvey
Jane Hissey
Anthony Horowitz
Lesley Howarth
Janni Howker
Roderick Hunt
Pat Hutchins

Rose Impey

Curtis Jobling
Terry Jones
Ann Jungman

Jackie Kay
Dick King-Smith

Robert Leeson
Joan Lingard
Penelope Lively

Wes Magee
Margaret Mahy
Jan Mark
Geraldine McCaughrean
Roger McGough
Adrian Mitchell
Tony Mitton
Bel Mooney
Michael Morpurgo
Brian Moses

Beverley Naidoo
Judith Nicholls
William Nicholson
Jenny Nimmo

Jan Ormerod
Gareth Owen

Brian Patten
Korky Paul

Gervase Phinn
Jan Pieńkowski
Chris Powling
Philip Pullman

Jane Ray
Shoo Rayner
John Rice
Chris Riddell
Philip Ridley
Tony Ross

Nick Sharratt
Posy Simmonds
Paul Stewart
Jeremy Strong
Jonathan Stroud
Robert Swindells

Nick Toczek
John Rowe Townsend
Hazel Townson

Kaye Umansky
Jean Ure

Martin Waddell
Nick Warburton
Colin West
Brian Wildsmith
Jacqueline Wilson

Benjamin Zephaniah

Joan Aiken

READING ALOUD WAS A DAILY HABIT in our family. My mother read aloud to me; she also read to my brother (12 years older) and to my sister (7 years older). My brother read aloud to my sister; she read aloud to me. My stepfather and my mother read to each other; evening by evening they worked through *War and Peace* or the *Journals* of André Gide, or all the Barchester novels. And I, as soon as I was old enough to do so, read aloud to anyone who would listen; my mother and I plugged our way steadily through the Bible, one of us reading and the other slicing beans (or whatever); besides this we used, all of us, sometimes to have Reading Tea, when every member of the family was allowed to bring a book to the table and silently munch while turning the pages. (This happened only when my stepfather had gone out for the day, however; he was something of a gourmet, and had too much respect for food to permit such an anti-social distraction from it). And, of course, we all read to my younger brother, who was seven years my junior.

These various threads of reading aloud made, I now see, a very interesting and comfortable series of extra connections throughout the family. It was as if we all met on a whole system of different interlocking levels.

Date and place of birth:
4th September 1924
Rye, Sussex
Contact address:
The Hermitage
East Street, Petworth
West Sussex GU28 0AB

Selected titles

The Wolves of Willoughby Chase (Red Fox)

Black Hearts in Battersea (Red Fox)

Go Saddle the Sea (Red Fox)

A Harp of Fishbones (Hodder Children's Books)

The Shadow Guests (Red Fox)

Extract

Many remember the learned professor
who lived in a cave on the cliff
adopted two whitethroats (one greater, one
    lesser)
and rowed them around in a skiff
and was writing a book about *If* …

Oh, many remember this learned old person
who knew such a lot about words
whose history of *But* no review was adverse on
who took such kind care of the birds
(he fed them on currants and curds)

Oh, many remember how once in October
the wind was beginning to moan
as he rambled the foreshore, abstracted and
    sober,
he picked up a page that had blown
down the shingle from sources unknown:

From 'If', *The Skin Spinners* (Viking)

Favourite book: *Persuasion* by Jane Austen
Favourite colour: Green
Favourite food: Cheese
Favourite word: Lullaby
Favourite place: A reach of the Derwent River in County Durham – now disappeared.
Where do your ideas come from? Dreams, things that happen to me or to people I know, stories I read every day in newspapers, or just ideas that float in from things I see in the street, which are jotted down in dozens of little notebooks.
What else might you have been? A painter.

Joan Aiken

1

Jez Alborough

IF YOU LOOK AT MY BOOKS YOU WILL notice that many of them feature animals as characters. However, the stories are really about humans. I use animals because it's easier to see ourselves one step removed. Have you ever met anyone like Duck from the *Duck in the Truck* series?

I test my books on my wife and of course my editor. My editor sometimes tests them on colleagues. Sometimes you get so close to a book that you miss something obviously not right – fresh pairs of eyes are really useful. If a joke is really funny but someone points out that it gets in the way of the logic of a storyline then it gets cut.

My other great love is playing the guitar and recently I have started writing and recording some music of my own. I even wrote a theme tune for Duck when I found a particularly quacky sound on my keyboard. When Duck is animated I hope it can be used at the start of the programme.

Date and place of birth:
Kingston upon Thames, Surrey
Contact address:
Walker Books
87 Vauxhall Walk
London SE11 5HJ

Selected titles

Hug (Walker Books)

Duck in the Truck (HarperCollins)

Fix-it Duck (HarperCollins)

Captain Duck (HarperCollins)

Where's My Teddy? (Walker Books)

It's the Bear (Walker Books)

Illustration

From *Hug* (Walker Books)

Favourite book: *The House at Pooh Corner* by A.A. Milne

Favourite colour: Red

Favourite food: I love nearly all vegetarian food

Favourite word: There are so many – how about prang, piffle and discombobulate?

Favourite place: Any warm beach with big waves to watch

Where do your ideas come from? Books can start in a number of ways. It could be with an idea for a character, a story idea, a joke or a catchphrase. The stories are built up around one of these foundations.

Fix-it Duck inherited some rhymes from *Duck in the Truck* – in the character names and vehicles – but to this I added the catchphrase "This is a job for Fix-it Duck". I've just realised that this was a catchphrase that I've borrowed from my youth – didn't Superman used to say "This is a job for Superman" before he flew off into some disaster that needed his help? Duck couldn't be less like Superman but there is a subtle link.

What else might you have been? A musician.

Jez Alborough

Nicholas Allan

I WROTE FOUR NOVELS AT SCHOOL, my first when 14, about two boys who murder another boy in school. I used to write every evening in my parents' bedroom since I shared a small room with my three brothers until I was 18. I liked school because, as I was good at art and writing, I was allowed to break rules. I wore a black suit, like an undertaker or Mafia boss.

I always enjoyed reading. I liked Ant and Bee, then Tintin. Tintin introduced me to guns, telephones, whisky and cigarettes. *The Castafiore Emerald* was a revelation – that you can write a story in which nothing happens: exactly like life.

I like writing more than anything except champagne and gruel.

Date and place of birth:
11th December 1956
Brighton, East Sussex
Contact address:
Lambeth Tavern
49D Lambeth Walk
London SE11 6DN

Selected titles

Jesus' Christmas Party

The Hefty Fairy

The Magic Lavatory

Heaven

The Queen's Knickers

All published by Red Fox

Extract

I'm the fairy who's lumpy,
I'm lumpy, frumpy and dumpy.
I dance round the ring
Flapping my wings,
Going bumpety! Bumpety! Bumpety!

From my first book, *The Hefty Fairy* (Red Fox)

Favourite book: *The Sun also Rises* by Ernest Hemingway
Favourite colour: Champagne
Favourite food: Gruel
Favourite word: Champagne
Favourite place: King's College Hospital Cardiac Ward. Born with a heart defect, I've spent long periods in hospital. I had a heart operation at King's one spring. The ward was honey coloured with sun, the staff friendly. I woke up from the operation and asked for a bowl of porridge. I took a mouthful and fell unconscious. Best porridge I ever tasted.

Where do your ideas come from? I live in a top flat with a view of Big Ben. I work seven days a week, 9–12.30pm / 2–4pm. I sit at a table with sheets of white paper and a Monc Blanc fountain pen. Sheer boredom forces me to put something on the sheets of paper.
What else might you have been? A heart surgeon, like Surgeon Sally in my book *Hilltop Hospital*.

Nicholas Allan

David Almond

I GREW UP IN A BIG CATHOLIC FAMILY on Tyneside. I loved playing football in the fields, messing about in the scrubland above our town, helping my grandfather in his allotment, camping out with my friends.

I wrote stories as a boy and always knew that I wanted to be a writer. I loved our local library and dreamed of seeing my books on its shelves one day. My favourite books were the King Arthur stories by Roger Lancelyn Green and the fake Tibetan tales of Lobsang Rampa.

I've been a postman, an editor and a teacher. I once lived in a remote commune for a year. I'm now a full-time writer and I live in Newcastle with my family. I write at home, in a room that overlooks our small back garden.

Date and place of birth:
15th May
Newcastle upon Tyne
Contact address:
The Maggie Noach
Literary Agency
22 Dorville Crescent
London W6 0HJ
www.davidalmond.co.uk

Selected titles

Secret Heart

Counting Stars

Heaven Eyes

Kit's Wilderness

Skellig

All published by Hodder Children's Books

Extract

The tiger padded through the night. Joe Maloney smelt it, the hot, sour breath, the stench of its pelt. The odour crept through the streets, through his open window and into his dreams. He felt the animal wildness on his tongue, in his nostrils. The tiger moved as if it knew him, as if it was drawn to him. Joe heard its footpads on the stairs. He heard its long slow breath, the distant sighing in its lungs, the rattle in its throat. It came inside. It filled the bedroom. The huge head hung over him. The glittering cruel eyes stared into him. The hot tongue, harsh as sandpaper, licked his arm. The mouth was wide open, the curved teeth were poised to close on him. He prepared to die. Then someone somewhere called.
"Tiger! Tiger! Tiger! Tiger!"
And it was gone.

From *Secret Heart* (Hodder Children's Books)

Favourite book: *Moby Dick* by Herman Melville
Favourite colour: Blue
Favourite food: Pasta, pesto and parmesan
Favourite word: Hawthorn
Favourite place: Crackpot Hill in Swaledale, Yorks – a ruined lead mine in a wild and wonderful setting.
Where do your ideas come from? From memories, dreams, things I've been told, things I've seen, things I've read. I spend a lot of time scribbling in notebooks, playing with words, images, fragments of stories – this kind of play is very useful in getting ideas out of my head and onto paper.
What else might you have been? A dazzling midfielder for Newcastle United. An opera singer. An explorer. A sculptor. Fortunately, I love being a writer.

David Almond

Bernard Ashley

I GREW UP IN WORLD WAR 2 and went to 14 different primary schools. Later I went to secondary schools in Blackheath and Rochester. National Service followed – in the RAF I "flew" a Remington typewriter. I trained as a teacher and was head of three schools (not all at once!) before concentrating on writing full-time. I wrote throughout, starting with short stories. My first novel, *The Trouble with Donovan Croft*, was published in 1974. Thirteen novels and numerous shorter stories and picture-book texts followed.

I write in a small office at the back of the house, overlooking a London garden – or out there under a tree. I like to use a black-nibbed pen in hardback notebooks, and now the electronic stuff. I write and rewrite and rewrite; I dislike anyone seeing what I'm doing until I'm happy with it.

My wife and I have three sons and four grandchildren. I love to go off to research my books – that has taken me from Warsaw to Wormwood Scrubs.

I love the theatre (but never go late). I am on the board of Greenwich Theatre, and a member of the BAFTA children's film and TV awards committee.

Date and place of birth:
2nd April 1935, London
Contact address:
128 Heathwood Gardens
London SE7 8ER
bernard.ashley@virgin.net
www.bashley.com
Speaking of Books
9 Guildford Grove
London SE10 8JY
020 8692 4704

Selected titles

Revenge House (Orchard Books)

Little Soldier (Orchard Books)

Johnnie's Blitz (Puffin)

The Trouble with Donovan Croft (OUP)

Double the Love – picture book (Orchard Books)

Extract

Kaninda walked away from the blood and the bodies, cold shock shaking him in the heat of the sun. He'd plugged his arm, wound a headscarf of his mother's round it tight. He swayed across the grass and stumbled through the gap in the hedge, the way the soldiers had come cutting in – the steel gates still locked and useless. Smoke hazed over the city centre where buildings had been torched. Staring through wide dry eyes, Kaninda held his suffocated chameleon to his stomach and headed the other way because that was where the others were walking – a string of scared Kibu families on the road, their things balanced in bundles on their heads and slung over their pushed bicycles, trekking together to get away from the Yusulu.

From *Little Soldier* (Orchard Books)

Favourite book: *The Power and the Glory* by Graham Greene
Favourite colour: Translucent, dark blue; opaque, scarlet
Favourite food: Vanilla ice-cream
Favourite word: Peace
Favourite place: Anywhere where my family is laughing.
Where do your ideas come from? My ideas come from life around me: an image, an account in the press or on the TV, day dreaming "what if". I saw a young man racked with tears at a road crossing; he nearly got himself run over. Then I saw the road sign a few metres on – to the local hospital. That's the start of a story.
What else might you have been? I was – for 38 years – a teacher. But I should also have liked to be an actor/director.

Bernard Ashley

Nina Bawden

I WAS BORN IN A RATHER DULL SUBURB of East London. Nothing exciting seemed to happen in our street, no one ever shouted or screamed and you couldn't see inside the houses because everyone had thick lace curtains at the windows. But I knew from the books I had read that in real life people quarrelled, lost all their money, went to prison. So to make things more interesting I made up good stories about our neighbours. They might look like bank clerks, fishmongers, shoe-menders, but in my stories about them they became arsonists, thieves, murderers ...

This got me into a lot of trouble, as you can imagine. My mother said, "Nina, how can you tell such terrible lies!" I said, "They're just stories. Like in books." My mother said, "That's quite different."

So I decided to write my stories down.

Date and place of birth:
19th January 1925
London
Contact address:
22 Noel Road
Islington
London N1 8HA
ninakrak@talk21.com

Selected titles

Carrie's War

The Peppermint Pig

Granny the Pag

Off the Road

The Outside Child

All published by Puffin

Extract

Granny Greengrass had her finger chopped off at the butcher's. She had pointed to the place where she wanted the joint to be cut, but then she decided she wanted a bigger piece and pointed again. Unfortunately, Mr Grummett the butcher was already bringing his sharp chopper down. He chopped straight through her finger and it flew like a snapped twig into a pile of sawdust in the corner of the shop.

It was hard to tell who was more surprised, Granny Greengrass or the butcher. But she didn't blame him. She said, "I could never make up my mind and stick to it, Mr Grummett. It's always been my trouble."

From *The Peppermint Pig* (Puffin)

Favourite book: *The Hobbit* by J.R.R. Tolkien
Favourite colour: Red
Favourite food: Lobster
Favourite word: Serendipity
Favourite place: A valley in the Marches of Wales between Bishop's Castle and Churchstoke.
Where do your ideas come from? Everywhere. Stories my grandfather told me. People I have seen on the bus. Memories. Smells. Books I have read.

Conversations I have listened to. Dreams. From anywhere and everywhere.
What else might you have been? I would have liked to be an actor, an explorer, or someone who sweeps up the leaves in the park – but only on nice, warm, sunny days!

Ian Beck

I LIKED DRAWING AT SCHOOL and was encouraged to go to painting classes at my local art college. I spent the first 20 years of my career working for grown-ups.

I started illustrating and writing for children when I had my own children. (I have three children now, two boys and a girl, Lily, who features in my Teddy stories like *Lost in the Snow*.)

I work at home and get out to visit schools and libraries all over the country when I can.

I loved (and still love) the 'Just William' books by Richmal Crompton with the Thomas Henry drawings.

Date and place of birth:
17th August 1947
Hove, Sussex
Contact address:
Speaking of Books
Jan Powling
9 Guildford Grove
London SE10 8JY

Selected titles

Lost in the Snow (Scholastic Children's Books)

Picture Book (Scholastic Children's Books)

Home Before Dark (Scholastic Children's Books)

Peter and the Wolf (Transworld)

Five Little Ducks (Orchard Books)

Illustration

From *Picture Book* (Scholastic Children's Books)

Favourite book: *The Lost Domain* by Alain Fournier
Favourite colour: Blue
Favourite food: Sausage and mash
Favourite word: Rain
Favourite memory: My childhood by the sea
Where do your ideas come from? My ideas come from noticing things in everyday life, either with my own children or at schools and libraries – then building the idea into a possible story in pictures.
What else might you have been? I should like to have acted on the stage or sung in the opera.

Malorie Blackman

I'VE ALWAYS LOVED READING. Reading was not just fun, it also helped me to make sense of the world (or at least try to!). I started writing when I was 26 and had my first book published when I was 28.

We don't have any pets at the moment. Every day my daughter asks for a dog so I expect she'll wear me down eventually!

I work up in my attic where it's nice and quiet. It's a pain when the doorbell goes though. My favourite books as a child were the 'Narnia' books by C.S. Lewis. I read them over and over (except for *The Last Battle*, which I wasn't so keen on).

I dislike rude and intolerant people and love the sea.

Date and place of birth:
8th February 1962
London
Contact address:
PO Box 9
Beckenham
Kent BR3 3WR
malorie.b@ukgateway.net

Selected titles

Noughts and Crosses (Doubleday)

Pig-Heart Boy (Corgi)

Hacker (Corgi)

Whizziwig (Puffin)

I Want a Cuddle (Orchard Books)

Favourite book: *The Silver Chair* by C.S. Lewis
Favourite colour: All of them
Favourite food: Lamb and rice
Favourite word: Love
Favourite memory: Holding my daughter for the first time.
Where do your ideas come from? My ideas come from anywhere and everywhere: conversations, newspaper articles, things I see, things I hear, things I feel, things I want to talk about, things I don't want to talk about.
What else might you have been? I would have been involved in books in some way – maybe running my own bookshop or working in publishing.

Malorie Blackman

Extract

Confidence up, confidence down
Act like an angel, look like a clown,
Changing your mind, changing it back.
The quick recipe for a heart attack.

Smile at your blunders, laugh at my own.
This isn't right, I should be at home.
Under the duvet, safe from attack.
Changing your mind, changing it back.

Accident prone, but never you worry,
I'll tell you when you can leave in a hurry.
Making up ground for the sense that I lack.
Changing your mind, changing it back.

I've done it again; proved my reputation.
Is this sorrow ... or is it elation?
Statements once given I cannot retract,
Changing your mind, changing it back.

The notice I earn is diluted with patience,
The smiles that I give are the scorns I receive.
While I hold my breath and count to one hundred,
You'll tell me a tale I am sure to believe.

Fanciful feelings hiding a fool,
A cog that's not turning, a bottomless pool.
Lend me what's common of which you've a stack.
Then I'll change your mind and I won't change it back.

From *Pig-Heart Boy* (Corgi)

Tony Bradman

I ENJOYED SCHOOL, and particularly liked reading and writing. My favourite stories when I was very young were the 'Thomas the Tank Engine' series, and later on I loved historical stories by writers like Rosemary Sutcliff and Henry Treece. I was also a big fan of *The Hobbit* and *The Lord of the Rings* by J.R.R. Tolkien.

I did a lot of writing in my teens – mostly poetry – but it wasn't until I became a dad and started reading children's books to my own children that I realised I wanted to write for children myself. I started off with little rhymes and poems I wrote for my kids, then went on to write picture books, then stories. My biggest early success was Dilly the Dinosaur, and most of the Dilly stories were based on my own children!

I still love writing, and these days I'm writing longer stories – I've just finished the second novel in a trilogy about a football team. I live in an old house in London, where I have a study upstairs, and far too many books ... I still read three or four books a week (at least!) and can't stop buying them. I also visit lots of schools and like meeting kids ... especially if they've read any of my books and say nice things about them!

Date and place of birth:
22nd January 1954
London
Contact address:
175 Mackenzie Road
Beckenham
Kent BR3 4SE
tbradman@dillythedinosaur.
co.uk

Selected titles

Dilly and the Goody-Goody – for beginner readers (Mammoth)

The Frankenstein Teacher – for beginner readers (Corgi)

Daddy's Lullaby – for under 5s (Bloomsbury)

Under Pressure – for over 12s (Corgi, 2002)

Smile, Please! – poems for 5–8s (Puffin)

Extract

The Thing

See the teacher reel with horror!
Hear the children squeal and scream!
Watch them all retreat in terror ...
From The Thing that's not a dream!

Listen to the slimy sliding!
See The Thing emerge some more!
Feel the panic, watch them hiding ...
Could they make it to the door?

Is The Thing an alien creature?
Is that why the classroom froze?
No ... "Get a tissue!" said the teacher ...
The Thing had come ...
from Jason's nose!

From *Here Come the Heebie-Jeebies and Other Scary Poems* (Hodder Children's Books)

Favourite book: *The Eagle of the Ninth* by Rosemary Sutcliff
Favourite colour: Black
Favourite food: Fish
Favourite word: Doosha (the Russian word for soul)
Favourite place: San Francisco, the most beautiful city I've ever seen.
Favourite memory: Five memories – the day I got married, the three days my children (Emma, Helen and Tom) were born, the day my granddaughter (Lily-Rose) was born.

Where do your ideas come from? I get my ideas from everything – memories, things I see or hear or read, people I meet. It's choosing the right idea to develop into a poem or short story that's important – and how to do that is very mysterious and difficult.
What else might you have been? I would have liked to have been an actor or film director ... or a musician ... or a professional sportsman ... or a teacher!

Ruth Brown

I GREW UP IN DEVON, Germany and Bournemouth and went to school and college in Bournemouth, Birmingham and London. My husband Ken is also an illustrator and we have two sons and one grandson.

I have had twenty-eight books published. I have also illustrated six of the James Herriot picture books. I like walking, gardening, reading, travelling, tennis, music, cooking and shopping; and I do not like ironing, filling in forms, spiders or heights. Our pets have inspired some of my books; one of our cats was called Flossie and another Holly.

I am very lucky to be able to earn my living by writing and illustrating books. It means I can work at my own pace, in my own time and in my own house. Sometimes I work very hard – seven days a week – and then when I finish a book I can take a little time off before I start the next one.

The very hardest part of my job is thinking of a good idea, the writing is the next most difficult, and then doing the illustrations is the very best part of all.

Date and place of birth:
20th May 1941
Tiverton, Devon
Contact address
12 Kingfisher Court
Bridge Road
East Molesey
Surrey KT8 9HZ

Illustration

From *Our Cat Flossie* (Andersen Press/Red Fox)

Selected titles

A Dark, Dark Tale

Our Cat Flossie

Snail Trail

Tale of the Monstrous Toad

Ten Seeds

All published by Andersen Press/Red Fox

Favourite book: *Treasure Island* by R.L. Stevenson
Favourite colour: Blue
Favourite food: Cheese
Favourite word: Granny
Favourite place: The seaside – anywhere

Where do your ideas come from? Anywhere and nowhere.
What else might you have been? I cannot imagine! But probably looking after stray cats and dogs.

Anthony Browne

I SPENT THE EARLY YEARS OF MY LIFE in a pub in Yorkshire, drawing battle scenes, kicking a ball around with my brother and telling stories to customers about a character called Big Dum Tackle. I've no idea where he came from.

My first book was published in 1976 and it came about mostly by chance. I'd had various jobs – medical illustrator, advertising, and designing greetings cards – and working in children's books seemed to be just another thing to try. Thirty-three books later I'm still making them and I know that for me it's the best job in the world. As a child my favourite book was *Treasure Island* with magnificent illustrations by N.C. Wyeth.

I work in a studio in my garden and look forward every day to my two children coming home.

Date and place of birth:
11th September 1946
Sheffield
Contact address:
Walker Books
87 Vauxhall Walk
London SE11 5HJ
aetb@btinternet.com

Selected titles

Gorilla (Walker Books)

Changes (Walker Books)

Voices in the Park (Transworld)

Willy the Dreamer (Walker Books)

Zoo (Red Fox)

Illustration

From *Gorilla* (Walker Books)

Favourite book: *Where the Wild Things Are* by Maurice Sendak
Favourite colour: Blue
Favourite food: Mango
Favourite word: Joskin
Favourite place: Venezuela – I had an exhibition there and a wonderful visit: stunning landscapes and amazingly friendly people.

Where do your ideas come from? From my own childhood, stories people tell me, films, paintings, dreams, things I read – and from my imagination.
What else might you have been? I'm not sure what else I could do – perhaps I would have liked to make films.

Anthony Browne

Alex Brychta

I WAS BORN IN PRAGUE and lived in Czechoslovakia until the age of 12. With both parents artists, I grew up surrounded by pictures. I hated going to school there and often rebelled against the strict regime of the communist educational system. My personal liberation came with the 1968 Russian occupation of my homeland, when my family moved to London. Suddenly my enthusiasm for drawing was no longer suppressed and I was encouraged to study all aspects of visual art including painting, photography, animation and graphic design. I was able to illustrate my first book while still at school.

I now live with my wife Dina and children Dylan and Kelly in a village not far from London. I work in a studio with a huge window and a view of the garden. So far, we have no pets because we like to travel abroad a lot, but that may soon change. I like playing golf, especially with my friend Rod Hunt who writes the Oxford Reading Tree books. I also like computers and friends often use me as a technical helpline. I don't think I'll ever throw my pens and brushes away, though.

Date and place of birth:
13th January 1956
Prague, Czech Republic
Contact address:
Oxed
Oxford University Press
Children's Publicity
Great Clarendon Street
Oxford OX2 6DP
brychta@aol.com

Selected titles

When in Spain – my very first book illustrations (J.M. Dent)

1 to 10 and Back Again – first book I wrote and illustrated (Franklin Watts)

Bee Gees – The Legend (Quartet)

The Flying Machine – by Rod Hunt; one of my favourite Oxford Reading Tree Stories (OUP)

People Like That – my 294th book, which I am now illustrating (OUP)

Illustration

From *Pocket Money* (OUP)

Favourite book: *Oxford English Dictionary*
Favourite colour: I like them all
Favourite food: Plum dumplings with Wensleydale cheese
Favourite word: Royalties
Favourite place: Summer holiday 1999 in the Dordogne, France, where my children learned to swim.
Where do your ideas come from? I have a lot of ideas suggested by Rod Hunt, my author, but I also get inspiration from everything I see around me. On top of that, I have a pretty fertile imagination, which comes in handy when I am working on Biff, Chip and Kipper's magic key adventures.
What else might you have been? Not a scientist, that's for sure. At school I hated maths. I wanted to be a balloon pilot but I would probably have ended up working in advertising along with most of my college friends.

Alex Brychta

Eric Carle

AS FAR BACK AS I CAN REMEMBER I enjoyed drawing pictures. I always knew that I would like to be an artist. My father loved to draw and he drew well. Often he drew pictures for me. He was also a wonderful story-teller and told me stories of animals and insects. I didn't read much as a child but I loved to sit on my father's lap and listen to him read the funnies in the Sunday paper to me. And I loved to go with him on walks in the woods where he would teach me about the creatures, small and big, who lived in the forest.

Almost without any planning, I became an author and illustrator of books for children. I studied art and design in Germany and started my career as a graphic designer. Later, I was an art director for an advertising agency in New York. In the mid-1960s Bill Martin Jr saw an ad of a red lobster that I had designed and asked me to illustrate his book *Brown Bear, Brown Bear, What Do You See?* I was so inspired by this wonderful book! This opportunity changed my life.

More than 30 years later, I'm still making books and am also working on another exciting project: The Eric Carle Museum of Picture Book Art, scheduled to open in late 2002 in Amherst MA. We have just started to build its foundations. To find out more please visit our web site www.picturebookart.org.

Date and place of birth:
25th June 1929
Syracuse, New York, USA
Contact address:
PO Box 485
Northampton, MA
01060, USA
fanclub@eric-carle.com
www.eric-carle.com

Selected titles

The Very Hungry Caterpillar (Puffin)

Brown Bear, Brown Bear, What Do You See? (Puffin)

The Bad Tempered Ladybird (Puffin)

The Very Busy Spider (Hamish Hamilton)

The Very Lonely Firefly (Philomel Books)

Extract

When all was quiet,
the firefly flew through the
night flashing its light,
looking and searching again.
Then the very lonely firefly
saw what it had been looking
for …
A group of fireflies, flashing
their lights.
Now the firefly wasn't lonely
anymore.

**From *The Very Lonely Firefly*
(Philomel Books)**

Favourite book: *Leo the Late Bloomer* by Robert Kraus, illustrated by Jose Aruego
Favourite colour: All colours
Favourite food: Honey and chocolate
Favourite word: Friendship
Favourite place: The large sun-filled room, large sheets of paper, fat brushes and colourful paints of my first-grade classroom in Syracuse, New York.
Where do your ideas come from? A child once told me that ideas come from both your outside and your inside. I found that to be a perceptive and accurate comment. No doubt, what is outside and what is inside are the basic elements in constructing a story, creating a painting or composing a piece of music. Some ideas for my books have been there, inside me, for a long time and others just come to me quickly. I'll think about a design concept and I'll get a spark or the beginning of an idea that way. Usually it's a combination of a lot of things: memory, design, dreams, experiences, things I've seen or heard.

Humphrey Carpenter

I STARTED TO REALISE that I enjoyed writing when I was at school – I wrote a serial for the school magazine called *Andy in Latin-land* – but I never thought of doing it professionally. After university I joined the BBC, then left seven years later to write the authorised biography of J.R.R. Tolkien. Only when that was finished did I realise I had become a writer, and had to think of other books to write!

One of the first I wrote then was a children's book about the canals called *The Joshers*. It sank without a trace! But in 1983 I was asked to write what became the beginning of the 'Mr Majeika' series, and I'm now about to write the thirteenth book in the series – except that at present I have absolutely no idea what will be in it!

Date and place of birth:
29th April 1946
Oxford
Contact address:
Penguin UK
80 Strand
London WC2R 0RL

Selected titles

Mr Majeika

Mr Majeika and the Music Teacher

Mr Majeika and the Haunted Hotel

Mr Majeika and the School Inspector

Mr Majeika on the Internet

All published by Puffin

Extract

The sun was shining down through the leaves, but as Jody watched, the sky – or the little she could see of it – grew dark and there was a flash of lightning and a big clap of thunder, followed by a huge downpour of rain. And while the storm raged, a canoe suddenly came into sight up the river. It was being paddled by Mr Majeika.

From *Mr Majeika and the School Trip* (Puffin)

Favourite book: *Alice in Wonderland* by Lewis Carroll

Favourite colour: Black

Favourite food: Spaghetti

Favourite word: All the words in the dictionary

Favourite place: The birth of my two children (I was there)

Where do your ideas come from? I just work out my ideas in my head – it's the hardest part of each book. The actual writing is easy. Also my books for children are a bit of a holiday after the big biographies I write for adults.

What else might you have been? I also work as a radio presenter, and if I hadn't left the BBC to write about Tolkien, I'd probably have stayed in radio – I like it much more than television. But I'm also a musician (I play lots of big bass instruments) and for eight years I ran a band — so I might have done that instead of writing.

Dick Cate

MY LOVE OF STORIES AND POEMS began in my junior school. I used to love reading about knights and damsels, brave quests and bonnie lasses. My first stories were for the junior school magazine. I just went on from there.

I have an affinity with animals. I think I must be one. As a child I had a rabbit, guinea-pigs, dogs and budgies.

The road to literature for me started with *The Beano*, went on to *The Wizard*, and led all the way to *The Hotspur*.

Date and place of birth:
31st March 1932
Ferryhill, Co. Durham
Contact address:
Ashfield, 2 Bank Lane
Denby Dale, Huddersfield
HD8 8QP
01484 862449
DICKLIZCATE@hotmail

Selected titles

Bernard's Prize (Walker Books)

Bernard's Magic (Walker Books)

Rodney Penfold, Genius (Walker Books)

The Doomsday Diary of Ermengarde Hulke (Walker Books)

Willie Scrimshaw Saves the Planet (HarperCollins)

Extract

Bernard falls in love with Amelia Humon, nicknamed Attila the Hun:
"I think I've fallen in love," said Bernard.
"Hard cheese," said Sqmashy. "Anybody I know?"
"Attila the Hun."
"Fate worse than death!"
"I think it's her eyes. They're so blue and misty."
"What are you talking about? Attila's eyes aren't blue. I know because they give me the screaming abdabs."
"I saw them," said Bernard.
"Maybe you need specs."
"I'm wearing specs."
"Maybe you need better ones," said Sqmashy.
From *Bernard's Magic* (Walker Books)

Favourite book: *Moonfleet* by J.M. Falkner
Favourite colour: Red
Favourite food: Any
Favourite word: All are lovely
Favourite memory: First setting eyes on my wife.
Where do your ideas come from? My ideas come from all over the place, all the time. I don't seem to have any of my own. They often come at a highly inconvenient moment: when I'm shaving, in a place where there isn't a pen for 400 miles, or when I'm trying to deal with another 5,000 ideas.
What else might you have been? Difficult to say. I was a teacher for 30 years and on the whole enjoyed it. But I seem to be programmed to imagine people, places, stories, witty replies etc. I can't stop the flow. It goes on and on and on and on and on and on etc.

Dick Cate

Babette Cole

I WENT TO A CONVENT SCHOOL where most of my time was spent drawing pictures and writing stories. When I got fed up with school, I left and went to art school in Canterbury, leaving in 1973 with a first-class honours degree. I made friends with Peter Firmin and Oliver Postgate who were making children's TV programmes for the BBC. They gave me my first proper drawing job for 'Jackanory' and TV comics. Once I had some work published by the BBC, I could go to other publishers with my own books and finally got one published in 1976. It did very well. Since then I have written over seventy books. The most famous one is called *Mummy Laid an Egg*, which sold over a million copies.

I have lived in different parts of the world, like Africa and the West Indies. At present I live in Lincolnshire and in Tortola in the British Virgin Islands.

In England I have a stud farm where I breed show hunters which I ride myself. I have been riding show ponies and horses since I was 7. They win lots of prizes and I'm very good at riding side-saddle. I was intermediate side-saddle rider of the year in 1998!

Date and place of birth:
1950 Jersey, Channel Islands
Contact address:
www.babette-cole.com

Selected titles

Mummy Laid an Egg (Red Fox)

Dr Dog (Red Fox)

Hair in Funny Places (Jonathan Cape)

Beware of the Vet (Egmont)

Lady Lupin's Book of Etiquette (Hamish Hamilton)

Illustration

From *Lady Lupin's Book of Etiquette* (Hamish Hamilton)

Favourite book: *Alice in Wonderland* by Lewis Carroll

Favourite colour: Cerulian blue, the colour of the sea in Tortola

Favourite food: Pheasant

Where do your ideas come from? Anywhere and everywhere. Pictures and words come at the same time, like a film running through my head.

What else might you have been? I wanted to be a writer/illustrator for as long as I can remember. It was a third option to being a vet or a professional horsewoman.

Babette Cole

Helen Cooper

WHEN I WAS 2, my family moved to a strange place where you collected your milk in a can from the farm, and bears lived inside cupboards under the stairs. I liked Cumbria pretty well, although it rained a lot and there weren't enough kids to play with. There were compensations: beautiful countryside, ponies and lots of time to write stories, draw pictures, play the piano and read. It was a time when kids were given only a sensible amount of homework, so there was plenty of time for hobbies.

Just as well, because I've ended up making a living from drawing pictures and writing stories, playing the piano and reading. I trained as a music teacher. Then I played in a band and taught myself to illustrate. Since then I've moved to London, and I've illustrated another 15 picture books. I wrote most of them too.

Now I live with my husband, Ted Dewan, who also writes and illustrates books. We often go to America to visit the pumpkin piles, and the road signs, which I put in many of my pictures. We have a small daughter called Pandora, and when she gives me time I still write stories, draw pictures, play the piano and read. I hope I never have to stop.

Date and place of birth:
19th May 1963
London
Contact address:
www.wormworks.com

Selected titles

Tatty Ratty (Doubleday/Picture Corgi)

Pumpkin Soup (Doubleday/Picture Corgi)

The Baby who Wouldn't Go to Bed (Doubleday/Picture Corgi)

The Bear under the Stairs (Doubleday/Picture Corgi)

The House Cat (Scholastic Children's Books)

Illustration

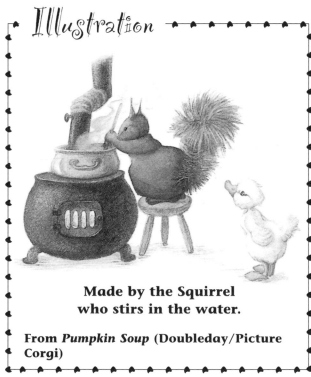

Made by the Squirrel who stirs in the water.

From *Pumpkin Soup* (Doubleday/Picture Corgi)

Favourite book: *Holes* by Louis Sachar
Favourite colour: Red
Favourite food: Potato and chocolate (not at the same time!)
Favourite word: Egg
Favourite place: The Rainbow Room on the top of the Rockefeller Center, New York.
Where do your ideas come from? Often my ideas come from things that happened to me when I was young. For instance, when I was 3 a bear came to live under our stairs.
What else might you have been? I'm grumpy when I'm not working on a book, so a very grumpy music teacher.

Susan Cooper

LIFE WAS VERY NOISY WHEN I WAS LITTLE, because it was World War 2 and aeroplanes were dropping bombs on our heads. Home was Buckinghamshire until I was 21, when my parents moved to my grandmother's family village of Aberdovey, in Wales. By that time I was working as a reporter in London and writing books in my spare time. But then I married an American and moved to Massachusetts, where eventually I had two children, Jonathan and Kate. When the children went to school in the morning, I'd start writing; when they came home again, I stopped.

The five books in 'The Dark is Rising' sequence are all set in my favourite childhood places: Buckinghamshire, Cornwall, Wales. Places are very important in my books: *Seaward* is a mix of England, Wales and Nevada; the Boggart books are Argyllshire and Toronto; *King of Shadows* is my beloved London. I always seem to write fantasies, I don't know why. Perhaps I write the kind of books I'd have liked to read when I was your age. I live in Connecticut now, and I'm married to the Canadian actor Hume Cronyn.

Date and place of birth:
23rd May 1935
Taplow, Buckinghamshire
Contact address:
missy.shef.ac.uk/~emp94ms

Selected titles

Over Sea, Under Stone – first of 5 books in 'The Dark is Rising', 8+ (Bodley Head/Puffin)

Dawn of Fear – World War 2 book, 10+ (Puffin)

The Boggart – fantasy, 8–12 (Bodley Head/Puffin)

King of Shadows – time travel, 10+ (Bodley Head/Puffin)

Green Boy – 8–12 (Bodley Head/Puffin)

Extract

As I watched, he began to walk slowly forward, over the mangrove-prickled sand, towards the shining stretches of the lagoon. It was a sort of measured walk, not the way a kid moves, and as he went, he did something even stranger, more adult – ancient, even. He raised both his skinny arms into the air, spread wide, as if he were going out to embrace someone.

He stood very still, just stood there, holding his arms out like that. It looked so weird, it sent a chill through me. I moved nervously up towards him, a few slow steps forward.

Then the sound all stopped, and the air wasn't shivering, and there was dead silence.

And out there in the lagoon the water seemed to open, and roll back and disappear. We stood there watching, scarce breathing, and a great shining city rose up before us, growing out of the earth.

From *Green Boy* (Bodley Head/Puffin)

Favourite book: *The Box of Delights* by John Masefield
Favourite colour: Blue-green
Favourite food: Peaches, raspberries, fishcakes (separately)
Favourite word: Dollop
Favourite place: My favourite childhood places.
Where do your ideas come from? Ideas come from a little room in the back of your head which has a locked door with no handle. Once in a while the door swings open of its own accord, and an idea runs out.
What else might you have been? A musician or a gardener.

Wendy Cope

WHEN I WAS A CHILD I USED TO WRITE STORIES in my spare time and say I wanted to be a writer. But I gave up on this ambition quite early and forgot all about it until I was in my late 20s. Then I suddenly began writing poems, and remembered that writing was what I had wanted to do.

I always liked reading. Sometimes my parents got fed up with me because I didn't seem to want to do much else. I hated all sport, except for swimming. In my teenage years I got very keen on music, playing the piano and singing in the school choir. At university I taught myself to play the guitar, which was useful when I became a primary school teacher.

The books I enjoyed as a child were school stories and horse stories and stories with dogs in them, such as *Greyfriars Bobby* and *Lassie Come Home*. And I remember liking *Little Women* and its sequels and *What Katy Did* and *Heidi*. I especially loved Kipling's 'Jungle Books'. The poetry we did at junior school was mainly about nature and fairies and I found it fairly boring. At secondary school I came across Yeats and Hardy and Wordsworth and Keats and Milton and realised that I could enjoy poetry after all.

Date and place of birth:
21st July 1945
Erith, Kent
Contact address:
Faber and Faber
3 Queen Square
London
WC1N 3AU

Selected titles

Twiddling Your Thumbs – hand rhymes for 2–6 years (Faber)

The River Girl – Narrative poem, 11+ (Faber)

Another Day on Your Foot and I would have Died – poems for children (with co-authors) (Macmillan Children's Books)

Making Cocoa for Kingsley Amis – collection of poems (Faber)

If I Don't Know – collection of poems (Faber)

Extract

Telling

One, two, three, four,
Telling Miss that Gary swore.
Five, six, seven, eight,
Now I haven't got a mate.

From *Twiddling Your Thumbs* (Faber)

Favourite book: *Persuasion* by Jane Austen
Favourite colour: Pink
Favourite food: Bread
Favourite word: Gobbledegook
Favourite place: Winchester, where I live now. The water meadows, the cathedral, our back garden.
Where do your ideas come from? My ideas come from things I read and things that happen in my life.
What else might you have been? I would probably have gone on being a primary school teacher.

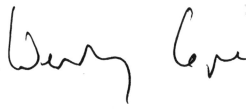

Pie Corbett

I WENT TO A VERY STRICT PRIMARY SCHOOL. My friend James was caned for eating an opal fruit! I always enjoyed stories – Mum or Dad read to me every night. Dad drove us to school and made up stories about a useless detective called Bracegirdle Bathwater! I had four brothers and we lived on a farm with dogs, ducks, chickens, goats and 27 cats.

As a schoolboy I was very shy and I thought that I was a dimwit. This was drummed into me – believing in yourself is very important. I write anywhere – at home I sometimes write in the garage where it is quiet and I have set up a desk. Sometimes I sit, staring into space waiting for a line to pop into my head. I think you have to learn how to listen for a poem, to listen to the storyteller in your head. Once I get an idea I follow it. At school I loved adventure stories, comics and Enid Blyton. I found poetry through the Liverpool Poets, T.S. Eliot, Ezra Pound and Ted Hughes.

Date and place of birth:
3rd April 1954
Hastings, East Sussex
Contact address:
Pipers Cottage
Oakridge Lynch
Stroud
Gloucestershire GL6 7NY
pikeorbit@tinyworld.co.uk

Selected titles

An Odd Kettle of Fish – poems with Brian Moses and John Rice (Macmillan Children's Books)

The King's Pyjamas – anthology for Key Stage I (Belitha)

The Apple Raid – anthology (Macmillan)

The Ramshackle Rainbow – anthology (Macmillan)

How to Write Chillers/Thrillers (Belitha)

Extract

Owl

Owl
was darker
than ebony
flew through the night
eyes like amber searchlights,
rested on a post,
feathers wind-ruffled,
stood stump still,
talons ready to seize
and squeeze.

Owl
was death
that swamped the fields
for it flew through the dark
that tightened its knot,
that bandaged the hills
in a blindfold of fever.

Owl flew – who – who – who

**From *An Odd Kettle of Fish*
(Macmillan Children's Books)**

Favourite book: *Skellig* by David Almond (at the moment)
Favourite colour: Blue
Favourite food: Boiled eggs – I've eaten a lot
Favourite word: Silence. (I like the word and the event.)
Favourite place: On top of the South Downs.
Where do your ideas come from? I write "diary" poems and these come straight from everyday experiences. I am very snoopy and always on the lookout for a good idea – I listen in on conversations, watch other people and also use memories. I keep writing journals where I jot ideas down – otherwise I'd forget them.

What else might you have been? I always wanted to be a comedian, because laughter makes everyone feel so good. I started out as a teacher and now write poems and tell stories. I did want to be a vet in Africa at one point – looking after lions and tigers, plucking thorns out of elephant's feet. I even had a British Airways timetable so I knew which flight I was going to catch (I was 7).

Pie Corbett.

Helen Cowcher

I GREW UP IN THE COUNTRYSIDE with two brothers. They both went to boarding school at 8 years of age, but I did not. My mother looked after us while my father worked. There was a large vegetable garden and soft fruits too, and an apple orchard. And the garden was surrounded by fields with cows and a horse. A stream ran past. We had lots of cats and a tree house in an old willow tree where one of the cats hid her new-born kittens.

I was inspired at school by my art teacher who was very strict and rather frightening, but also very encouraging and taught us a lot. I loved picture books, fairy stories and books about nature but often the animals in the books were dressed up in human clothes and not really wild animals, so unlike the books which I choose to write and illustrate now.

We didn't get a television until I was 11 years old, so the imaginative journeys I made when I was younger were all inspired by books – or sometimes by anecdotes which my father told. He used a lot of interesting words in his writing and speech and so I've always liked words and the sound of them.

Date and place of birth:
10th August 1957
Cheltenham, Gloucestershire
Contact address:
30 Telford Avenue
London SW2 4XF

Selected titles

Rainforest

Antarctica

Tigress

All published by Milet Ltd in dual language editions.

Whistling Thorn (Scholastic Children's Books/Milet Ltd/ Hippo)

Jaguar (Scholastic Children's Books/Milet Ltd/ Hippo)

Illustration

From *Jaguar* (Scholastic Children's Books/ Milet Ltd/Hippo)

Favourite book: *The Snowman* by Raymond Briggs

Favourite colours: White and black

Favourite food: Meringue

Favourite word: Elbow

Favourite place: Flood plains of the great Orinoco River, Venezuela, South America

Where do your ideas come from? My ideas come from anywhere – from travelling, from things I see, from reading newspapers, sometimes from television and radio, other books and my friends. The hard thing is to have a good idea.

What else might you have been? I am an artist too. But apart from that, I would have been a field biologist/zoologist/conservationist working in central or southern America on projects to help people and wilderness survive together sustainably.

Helen Cowcher

Helen Craig

AS I WAS A LITTLE CHILD DURING WORLD WAR 2 I did not have as many picture books as children today. But I had, and loved, the Beatrix Potter books, *Orlando the Marmalade Cat*, *Babar the Elephant* and my favourites 'The Little Grey Rabbit' series and the Sam Pig stories by Alison Uttley, so I didn't do too badly! I loved the world that the pictures seemed to invite me to enter – I always felt that I would discover more than was actually in the pictures if I looked really hard – and in a way I did because my imagination would take over. I had other books that belonged to my parents when they were children and I think these early books influenced me a lot.

Later, I found one of these old books in a second-hand bookshop and although it was expensive I simply had to buy it. Every illustration was full with memories of the feelings I had as a child when I had looked at them – every mark meant something to me even after so many years.

I am still looking for some of those old books and I am still reliving those feelings I had as a child when I do illustrations now.

Date and place of birth:
30th August 1934
London
Contact address:
Carole Heaton (Agent)
37 Goldhawk Road
London W12 8QQ
cheaton@greeneheaton.
co.uk

Selected titles

Angelina Ballerina – series by Katherine Holabird (Viking Children's Books)

This is the Bear – series by Sarah Hayes (Walker Books)

The Yellow House – by Blake Morrison (Walker Books)

The Town Mouse and the Country Mouse – rewritten/illustrated by Helen Craig (Walker Books)

The Orchard Nursery Story Book – illustrated by Helen Craig (Orchard Books)

Illustration

From *The Town Mouse and the Country Mouse* (Walker Books)

Favourite book: *Higglety Pigglety Pop* by Maurice Sendak

Favourite colour: Impossible – all colours!

Favourite food: Lobster

Favourite memory: My new-born baby son

Where do your ideas come from? I suppose ideas are a mixture of all things you have seen that are stored up in your memory. Some artists like to work from actual models and places. I enjoy inventing – I prefer to use my imagination. I like to go into the world I am creating on the paper and let my imagination take over.

What else might you have been? I've often thought it would be wonderful to be a musician. Or it might be fun to be a racing driver!

Helen Cresswell

MY MOTHER TAUGHT ME TO READ when I was 4 and from then on I read greedily. I started writing poems and stories at around 6 and still have some of the early pieces in an old ledger. I loved fairy stories and folk tales best, I think, and was soon reading all my mother's books, from the novels of Thomas Hardy (my favourite) to the poetry of Keats and Shelley. I used to write sitting on my bed; nowadays I have a study lined with books and write books and TV scripts sitting on the floor. I write in longhand because I love the feeling, in plain A4 hardback books, using a pen with proper, flowing ink. (Brown ink for fantasy, black for TV or anything funny.)

Date and place of birth:
11th July 1934
Sutton-in-Ashfield
Nottinghamshire
Contact address:
Old Church Farm
Eaksing
Newark
Nottinghamshire
NG22 0DA

Selected titles

Moondial (Puffin)   The Bagthorpe Saga – 10 titles (Hodder Children's Books)

The Piemakers (OUP)   A Gift From Winklesea – 3 books (Hodder Children's Books)

Snatchers (Hodder Children's Books)

Extract

She had a curious sense of being drawn, of having no choice. As she went she was taking steps that had already been measured for her. She lifted her eyes and saw ahead, at the crossroads of the garden, another statue, and felt a prickling of her shoulderblades. There was a power in the air, so strong that she could hardly breathe.

Minty stopped in front of the statue, with icy tides washing her from head to foot. There were an old man and a young boy, both winged like angels, though she was certain that they were not. They seemed to be wrestling, struggling for possession of a bowl above their heads and, catching a glimpse of a metal beak, Minty suddenly realized what it was.

"A sundial!" she exclaimed softly, and then, almost immediately and without knowing why – "Moondial!"

And as she spoke the word a cold distinct wind rushed past her and the whole garden stirred and her ears were filled with a thousand urgent voices. She stood swaying. She put her hands over her ears and shut her eyes tight.

From *Moondial* (Puffin)

Favourite book: *The Wind in the Willows* by Kenneth Grahame

Favourite colour: Blue

Favourite food: Roast beef and Yorkshire pudding

Favourite word: Estuary (close second: epiphany)

Favourite memory: My favourite memory is of a darkening beach on the east coast, shoring up sandcastles against the crashing rollers.

Where do your ideas come from? I do a lot of day-dreaming (I think it should be in the National Curriculum) and ideas often come then, or while I'm walking, or they could come from something I've seen on TV or in a newspaper – anywhere!

What else might you have been? I'd have liked to be an actress or a painter – I do paint in my spare time. But I can't really imagine being anything but a writer.

Helen Cresswell

Gillian Cross

I GREW UP IN A HOUSE with a big garden. I loved to wander round it and stare at the plants. I still like staring at plants. I liked reading *The Secret Garden*, *Little Women*, the Arthur Ransome books and lots of Shakespeare and Enid Blyton.

I have always written the beginnings of books and made little books, which I sewed together. I didn't finish a full-length book until I was about 28. Since then, I have written at least one book every year.

I work in a little room behind the kitchen. It has a table, two chairs and a filing cabinet in it, and also a ludicrous number of books. All I can see through the window is a brick wall and that's how I like it. A view would be distracting, but I don't like rooms without windows.

Date and place of birth:
24th December 1945
Wembley, London
Contact address:
Oxford University Press
Children's Publicity
Great Clarendon Street
Oxford OX2 6DP
www.gilliancross.co.uk

Selected titles

The Demon Headmaster
(Puffin)

Wolf (OUP)

The Great Elephant Chase
(OUP)

Calling a Dead Man (OUP)

Beware Olga! (Walker Books)

Extract

He came in the early morning, at about half past two. His feet padded along the balcony, slinking silently past the closed doors of the other flats. No one glimpsed his shadow flickering across the curtain or noticed the uneven rhythm of his steps.

But he woke Cassy. She lay in her bed under the window and listened as the footsteps stopped outside. There were two quick, light taps on the front door. Then a pause and then two more taps, like a signal.

Cassy sat up slowly. She heard the door of the back room open and Nan come hurrying out. Not running (nurses never run, except for fire or haemorrhage), but crossing the tiny hall in two quick strides.

The front door handle clicked, but no one spoke and no light from the hall showed under Cassy's door. He came in quickly, in silence, in the dark, and the door closed behind him at once.

From *Wolf* (OUP)

Favourite book: *The Secret Garden* by Frances Hodgson Burnett
Favourite colour: Green
Favourite food: Thick vegetable soup
Favourite word: I haven't got a favourite word. It's the way they work together that I like.
Favourite place: Castlerigg stone circle
Where do your ideas come from? I usually get a little snippet of an idea – like the trailer for a film – and I write the book to discover what it is all about. But I haven't the faintest idea where the snippet comes from.
What else might you have been? If I hadn't been a published writer, I would have been an unpublished writer. I like to spend a lot of time on my own so maybe I could have been a lighthouse keeper (if they hadn't all gone automatic!).

Gillian Cross

Kevin Crossley-Holland

I DIDN'T READ MUCH AS A BOY, and the only library book I ever borrowed I kept for far, far too long. Forty years! What I loved best was heading off into the beechwoods (in the Chiltern Hills) with my bull terrier, Bruce; and spending hours and hours in my museum shed amongst my treasures – fossils, potsherds, coins (including the Roman one I found myself), and a marvellous crusader shield. For our holidays, my sister Sally (three years younger than I) and I often used to visit my grandparents on the north Norfolk coast. That's where Linda (my Minnesotan wife) and I live now, in a little wind-whipped seventeenth-century cottage – and my ghost story *Storm* as well as many of my poems are set around here.

In *The Seeing Stone* and *At the Crossing-Places*, I've drawn deeply on the events and sounds, sights, tastes, smells of my own childhood. Sitting in my little study, and writing (left-handed) with my old pen, I'm living in several layers: here and now, my childhood, medieval times ... My old school motto was *Et nova et vetera*: both new and old. And that's what we all are, if we stop to think about it.

Date and place of birth:
7th February 1941
Mursley, Buckinghamshire
Contact address:
Orion Children's Books
Orion House
5 Upper St Martin's Lane
London WC2H 9EA

Selected titles

The Seeing Stone – first part of 'Arthur' trilogy (Orion Children's Books)

At the Crossing-Places – second part of 'Arthur' trilogy (Orion Children's Books)

The Magic Lands – British folk-tales (Orion Children's Books)

Short! – 44 very short stories (OUP)

The Green Children – illustrated by Alan Marks (OUP)

Extract

Tumber Hill! It's my clamber-and-tumble-and-beech-and–bramble hill! Sometimes, when I'm standing on the top, I fill my lungs with air and I shout. I shout ...
When I climbed the hill this afternoon, I saw Merlin already sitting on the crown, and the hounds bounded ahead of me and mobbed him.
Merlin tried to swat them away with the backs of his spotty hands, and scrambled to his feet. "Get away from me!" he shouted. "You creatures!"
"Merlin!" I called out, and I pointed to the sky's peak. "Look at that cloud."
"I was," said Merlin.
"It's a silver sword. The sword of a giant king."
"Once," said Merlin, "there was a king with your name."
From *The Seeing Stone* – first part of 'Arthur' trilogy (Orion Children's Books)

Favourite books: Myths, legends and folk-tales
Favourite colour: Purple
Favourite food: Summer pudding
Favourite word: Maybe 'keen', maybe 'onomatopoeia'
Favourite memory: A saltwater creek at low tide, the shrimping pools tepid, wet sand between my toes, gulls mewing, deep breathing of the marsh. Now the wind picks up, the silver-dark tide turns and quickens ...
Where do your ideas come from? Watching people, listening to people, especially children; history, especially the Middle Ages, the music of language; now and then "unhurrying", looking out of the window and beginning to dream.
What else might you have been? I wanted to be a sports commentator, then a cricketer, then an archaeologist, then a priest. I have been a publisher, briefly a BBC talks producer, a broadcaster, and a professor.

Kevin Crossley-Holland

Colin Dann

I GREW UP IN A LONDON SUBURB but I was fortunate to have a wealth of parks and commons and also the riverside on my doorstep. So I was able to observe nature – and to daydream about it – early in life. My parents devoured and hoarded books and I took after them. From the age of 8 or 9 I began to write little stories. One of these won a prize in an RSPCA essay competition.

Later my brother and I used to write weird or comic verse and tales and read them to each other, collapsing into fits of laughter. I started to write with a view to publication when I was 19 but I had to wait a long time before I was successful! My first book, *The Animals of Farthing Wood*, was published when I was in my early 30s. I still write regularly and try to reach a target of a certain number of words each day. I have always written in pencil initially (easy to revise!). I type the story later as I polish it up.

For the last sixteen years I've lived with my wife in Sussex, at present in a converted oast house on the Sussex/Kent borders. The countryside around is beautiful and very varied. It is a tremendous inspiration to me.

Date and place of birth:
10th March 1943
Richmond, Surrey
Contact address:
Random House Children's Books
61–66 Uxbridge Road
Ealing
London W5 5SA

Selected titles

The Animals of Farthing Wood (Mammoth)

The Fox Cub (Red Fox)

The Beach Dogs (Red Fox)

The City Cats (Red Fox)

Lion Country (Red Fox)

Extract

Toad led them upstream a short way, looking carefully for the spot where he himself had crossed before. Eventually he came to a halt.
"I'm sure this is it," he told them confidently.
"There's a hole in the bank here just like the one I hid in last time. It must be the same one."
The animals drew themselves up into a bunch, and all of them started to jostle at the water's edge in their efforts to examine the state of the river.
"You're right, Toad," Fox declared. "The water here seems scarcely to be moving."
"It looks a long way to the other bank," squeaked Fieldmouse.
"Don't worry," said Toad kindly. "I'll go across first. You can watch me. I'm about your size, and if I can do it …"

From *The Animals of Farthing Wood* (Mammoth)

Favourite book: *The Count of Monte Cristo* by Alexandre Dumas
Favourite colour: Green
Favourite food: Roast beef
Favourite word: Laughter
Favourite place: Richmond Park
Where do your ideas come from? From almost anywhere, but mainly from observing life in the countryside – the life, that is, of its smaller inhabitants, the original ones who have always been there, long before humans arrived on the scene.
What else might you have been? Something to do with books – I worked in publishing for many years before becoming a professional writer. I can't imagine myself without that book connection in some way.

Colin Dann

Peter Dixon

I DIDN'T LIKE READING AND WRITING when I was at school. I couldn't spell, understand adverbs or do comprehension exercises properly. I did write at home (secretly), but never showed people what I had written in case they said it was all wrong.

I can't remember my mum or dad reading to me very much either, and I don't think I ever really wanted them to ... Anyway my dad was away fighting Hitler and he was in a prisoner-of-war camp. (He wasn't really, but I always told people he was.)

I do remember my lovely mum, however. She was a brilliant mother and often used to take her false teeth out and chase us around the house pretending to be a witch. It seemed better than being read to.

I loved going out to play and boxing much more than books – although *The Beano* and *Dandy* were OK. The clever kids read "sensible" comics like *The Eagle* but I didn't.

Wife? Just the one and two children (one of each kind). House? – Yes, with posh front gates and a dad who is 96. Hello, Dad!

Before becoming a full-time writer I was a senior lecturer in education. I don't quite know how I got a smart job like that. I just did.

Date and place of birth:
6th April 1937, London
Contact address:
30 Cheriton Road
Winchester
Hampshire SO22 5AX
01962 854 607

Favourite book: *Just William* by Richmal Crompton
Favourite colour: Grey
Favourite food: Crackle on pork
Favourite word: Macmillan
Favourite place: Whitby, where I spent lots of my childhood getting wet.

Where do your ideas come from? Rusty tins and funny faces,
Pretty gardens, ugly places.
Dogs and cats and kangaroos,
People's socks and people's shoes.
Tears and sadness – people starving –
Killing sharks (DON'T!) ...
and, well, just anything other than spring, bonfire night and windy days. I don't write about things that there are already hundreds of poems about.

What else might you have been? If it wasn't wicked and bad and wrong and awful, I'd have been a burglar. It must be fun creeping about in dark houses – sorting through things. But I can't. And neither can you! So I suppose my second thing would be either a Harrier pilot or a beachcomber.

Peter Dixon

Extract

Roger's Daddy's clever
Daisy's flies a plane
Michael's does computers
And has a house in Spain.
Lucy's goes to London
He stays there every week ...
    But my Daddy has an earring
      and lovely dancing feet.

He hasn't got a briefcase
He hasn't got a phone
He hasn't got a mortgage
And we haven't got a home.
He hasn't got a fax machine
We haven't got a car
    But he can dance and fiddle
    And my Daddy is
    A Star.
From *Peter Dixon's Poetry Grand Prix* (Macmillan Children's Books)

Selected titles

Grow Your Own Poems (Peche Luna)

The Colour of my Dreams (Macmillan Children's Books)

Peter Dixon's Poetry Grand Prix (Macmillan Children's Books)

Penguin in the Fridge (Macmillan Children's Books)

Juggler (Barrington Stoke)

Berlie Doherty

WHEN I WAS 4 we moved from Liverpool to a little seaside town called Hoylake, in the Wirral. My first school was near the sea, and I used to play in the sandhills on the way home, or go swimming with my dad. I was always writing stories and poems and sometimes had them illustrated by my friends or published in the local paper. One of my first stories was about my cat, Kim. I've always had cats. I wrote a book called Paddiwak and Cosy about two of my cats, and my present cat is called Midnight, because he has a black coat with a white moon under his chin and a white star at the end of his tail.

I used to write my stories in a little bay called Red Rocks, but now I have a barn which looks out over the Pennines, fields of sheep, and Star, the pony who belongs to the children next door. I like to play my tin whistle while I'm thinking about what to write next.

Date and place of birth:
6th November
Knotty Ash, Liverpool
Contact address:
Jacqueline Korn (agent)
David Higham Associates
5–8 Lower John Street
Golden Square
London W1R 4HA
www.berliedoherty.com

Selected titles

Fairy Tales – illustrated by Jane Ray (Walker Books)

Children of Winter (Mammoth)

Snowy – illustrated by Keith Bowen (Collins)

Midnight Man – illustrated by Ian Andrew (Walker Books)

Coconut Comes to School – illustrated by Ivan Bates (Collins)

Zzaap and the Word Master (BBC Publications)

Extract

Mother Greenwood took the belt from Jill and ran her fingers over the lettering, mumbling words that Jill couldn't understand. "What does it say?" Jill asked, but old Mother Greenwood shook her head and closed her eyes as if she was hugging great secrets to herself. "It's a language of long ago, that the Cornish folk used to speak. You won't be ready to read that yet."
"Does it belong to Jack? Is there a story about it?"
"Of course there's a story about it. There's a story about everything … but" the old woman shook her head. "It's not for you. Not at this time of night. Why, it would frighten the life out of you. Look at the cat, skimbled out of his wits. No, it's not for you, that tale." She hung the belt on a hook by the fire, where it swung backwards and forwards like the pendulum of a clock. Tick, tick, tock, tock, and the griffin's head buckle gleamed like the sun itself. From his safe place on the top shelf of the dresser the cat watched it, his head swinging in time to its rhythm.
From *The Famous Adventures of Jack* (Hodder Children's Books)

Favourite book: 'The Stone Book Quartet' by Alan Garner
Favourite colour: Blue
Favourite food: Mashed potato and onion gravy
Favourite word: Lullaby
Favourite place: The beautiful valley where I live
Where do your ideas come from? Anywhere and everywhere. I got the idea for *Willa and Old Miss Annie* because I thought I saw a ghost in my friend Willa's garden one night. I got the idea for *Daughter of the Sea* when I was a little girl, and I used to swim with the seals.

What else might you have been? I had a list of things I would like to be: writer (yes!), singer (I sang with a folk duo for eight years), librarian (I had a job shelving books when I was 16), ballet dancer (never even had lessons!), swimming pool attendant (never made it!), or air hostess.

Anne Fine

I QUITE LIKED SCHOOL, so long as I was left alone. (The words I hated to hear the most were "Now choose a partner.") I liked English. But it was very different in those days. You didn't have to share and discuss your ideas. You didn't have to plan, or draft. You were just allowed to choose between four or five titles and sit there quietly getting on with it. (I think that was much better.)

I wrote *pages*. I'd hide my work with my arms if anyone came near. And I did get good marks.

I read all the time. (Still the very best practice for being a writer.) I had my own library tickets and my friends' tickets and the lady next door let me use her tickets too. The librarians all knew me. "Look. Here she is again. Wasn't she in here this morning? Does she do nothing else but read?"

And the answer was – No. She didn't.

Date and place of birth:
7th December 1947
Leicester
Contact address:
www.annefine.co.uk

Selected titles

Loudmouth Louis –
7–10 years (Puffin)

The Angel of Nitshill Road –
7–11 years (Mammoth)

Care of Henry –
6–9 years (Walker Books)

Step by Wicked Step –
9–12 years (Puffin)

Crummy Mummy and Me –
8–12 years (Puffin)

Extract

I don't think my mum's fit to be a parent, really I don't. Every morning it's the same, every single morning. I'm standing by the front door with my coat on, ready to go. School starts at nine and it's already eight-forty or even later, and she's not ready. She's not even nearly ready. Sometimes she isn't even dressed.
"Come *on*," I shout up the stairs. "We have to leave now."
"Hang on a minute!"
"What are you *doing* up there?" Her voice comes, all muffled, through the bedroom door:
"Nothing."
"You *must* be doing something,"
I yell.
"I'm *not*."
"Come down, then. We're *waiting*."
"Can't find my shoes."
I lean against the front door, sighing. With as much patience as I can muster, I call upstairs: "Where did you take them off?"
"I *thought* I took them off in the bathroom …"
"Look there, then."
"I *have*."
"If you would only put your shoes away neatly at night, we wouldn't have to go through this every single morning!"
From *Crummy Mummy and Me* (Puffin)

Favourite book: *Vanity Fair* by William Thackeray
Favourite colour: Green
Favourite food: Toasted cheese
Favourite word: Silver
Favourite place: A hot bath (reading)
Where do your ideas come from? Ideas are all around. The secret is knowing what you can do with them. Is it just a tiny idea that could make up a poem, or a tiny part of a story about something

else? Or is it a huge idea that will keep you going for pages and pages? You soon learn which.
What else might you have been? I'd probably have tried to find some job where reading counts. So maybe a librarian. Or a publisher's reader. (That's the person who reads all the books sent to a publisher to see if they're good enough to be published.) Or maybe I'd have been a translator, changing someone's Spanish novels into English.

Catherine Fisher

AROUND THE CORNER from where I lived when I was small was a tiny branch library in a rainy street, and there I read *Treasure Island*, the Alice books, all the 'Just William' stories and a series of books of the folktales and myths of various countries.

Later came King Arthur, and Robin Hood and Sherlock Holmes, and the Mabinogi. These must be the basic ingredients of anything that I've written since.

I began writing poetry at 11 but stories came much later, when I went to college. I write longhand, sometimes to music, with my two cats Jesse and Tam Lin sleeping on their paws nearby.

I like woods, trees, folk music, Led Zep, drawing and geraniums.

Date and place of birth:
Newport, Gwent,
South Wales
Contact address:
Laurence Pollinger Ltd
9 Staple Inn, Holborn
London WCIV 7QH
www.LaurencePollinger.com
www.geocities.com/
catherinefisheruk

Selected titles

The Book of the Crow – fantasy quartet (Red Fox)

Darkwater Hall (Hodder Children's Books)

The Lammas Field (Hodder Children's Books)

The Snow-Walker Trilogy (Red Fox)

Belin's Hall (Red Fox)

All fantasy/sci-fi novels for 12+

Extract

Galen looked up and pointed at the dwarf. "Hear me" he said, the darkness rustling around him, his voice shaking with effort. "In the name of the Makers, I curse you, thief-lord. I curse you up and down, from side to side, from front to back. I curse you from fingertip to fingertip, head to toe. I curse you today and yesterday and tomorrow. I curse all you eat, all you drink, all you speak, all you dream."
White-faced, the dwarf stared up at him. The cave was black, crackling with power. The fire went out, and still Galen snarled the words remorselessly, his finger pointed, sparks leaping about it.
"May your possessions be dust to you. May your body tremble and rot. May your hair turn white and fall …"
"No." Alberic stepped back, holding up his hands. "No! Wait!"

From *The Interrex* (vol. 2 of 'The Book of the Crow') (Red Fox)

Favourite book: *The Lord of the Rings* by J.R.R. Tolkien
Favourite colour: Green
Favourite food: Chocolate
Favourite word: Menelaos – or cyfeillion (Welsh for 'friends')
Favourite place: The Ridgeway, Wiltshire
Where do your ideas come from? My ideas come from myths and legends, and from places. The most charged places have legends about them. Gwent is full of places like that.
What else might you have been? An archaeologist.

Pauline Fisk

I STARTED WRITING AT THE AGE OF 9, inspired by a love of Winnie the Pooh. I had been telling stories for years, but it was when I started writing them down that I decided to become a writer when I grew up.

Apart from daydreaming on the back row and writing stories and poems, there was very little that I liked about school. I grew up in London, but moved to Shropshire when I was in my mid-20s.

I have five grown-up children and I love being a mum. My husband is an architect, and we both enjoy art, music, films, drama, and walking in the country and by the sea. Our family dog is a small, hairy terrier called Biffo.

Books I enjoyed as a child include Hans Christian Andersen's fairy tales, Alan Garner's *Weirdstone of Brisingamen* and Tolkien's *The Hobbit*. Books I enjoy as an adult include the novels of Graham Greene, Ella Maillart's *Forbidden Journey* about an amazing journey across China, and the Australian writer Tim Winton's *Cloudstreet*.

I work in my bedroom at a desk by my bed, humming along with the rhythm of my writing to make my stories sound right.

Date and place of birth:
27th September 1948
London
Contact address:
Laura Cecil Agency
17 Alwyne Villas
London
N1 2HG

Selected titles

Midnight Blue (Lion Publishing)

Telling the Sea (Lion Publishing)

Sabrina Fludde (Bloomsbury Children's Books)

The Beast of Whixall Moss (Walker Books)

The Candle House (Bodley Head)

Extract

This was the moment when the river ended and the sea began. The moment which Abren had waited for. She threw away her paddle and took Phaze ll's hands. Moved out into the sea, and its waves leapt under her like wild white horses. The air was clear and heady, like vintage sea wine, and Abren could hear "her" tune again. *Hear it playing for the dance.*

She sang along with it, word for word. Tapped her toes and beat time. The sun went down and the moon rose in the sky. The waves began to race, and she felt the pull of a new horizon drawing her across the sea. A new adventure steering her beneath the stars.

Phaze ll glanced at her as if to say that he could feel it too.

From *Sabrina Fludde* (Bloomsbury Children's Books)

Favourite book: *A Hundred Years of Solitude* by Gabriel Garcia Marquez
Favourite colour: Sometimes red, sometimes blue, never black.
Favourite food: Homemade bread
Favourite word: Yes
Favourite place: Dinas Head, Pembrokeshire
Where do your ideas come from? Places that I love; good conversation; good books, poems and paintings and pieces of music; long walks; hard thinking; dreams; newspaper items; sounds and smells and anything that moves. Mostly, ideas come from loving life and wanting to know more about it, from asking questions and believing in the impossible.
What else might you have been? There's nothing else I wanted to be.

John Foster

I'VE ALWAYS LOVED WORDS and English was one of my favourite subjects at school, so I suppose it's not surprising that I eventually became a writer. I'm also keen on sport, and I spent a lot of my childhood playing games – cricket and tennis especially. I dreamed of playing cricket for England, but the furthest I ever got was opening the batting for Carlisle in the North Lancashire League.

I enjoyed reading and my parents let me read whatever I wanted. My favourite stories were the football stories in comics, such as *The Wizard* and *The Hotspur* and a series of cowboy books about Roy Rogers. I liked reading poetry, too. My favourite book was *The Dragon Book of Verse*.

There weren't as many poetry books for children then as there are now and I'm lucky enough to have been one of the people involved in what I call the "children's poetry revolution". When I'm not writing my own poems or out and about performing them, I spend my time selecting poems for new anthologies. I've lost count of how many anthologies I've done – it's well over a hundred now.

Date and place of birth:
12th October 1941
Carlisle, Cumbria
Contact address:
Oxford University Press
Children's Publicity
Great Clarendon Street
Oxford OX2 6DP

Selected titles

Four O'clock Friday – collection of original poems, 7–11 years (OUP)

Twinkle, Twinkle, Chocolate Bar – anthology of rhymes, 3–7 years (OUP)

Firewords – anthology of wordplay poems, 7–11 years (OUP)

Dinosaur Poems – one of series of anthologies for 5–9 years illustrated by Korky Paul (OUP)

A Century of Children's Poems – collection of 100 poems by leading 20th-century children's poets (Collins)

Extract

Children's Prayer

Let the teachers of our class
Set us tests that we all pass.
Let them never ever care
About what uniform we wear.
Let them always clearly state:
It's OK if our homework's late.
Let them say it doesn't matter
When we want to talk and chatter.

Let our teachers shrug and grin
When we make an awful din.
Let them tell us every day
There are no lessons. Go and play.
Let them tell our mum and dad
We're always good and never bad,
Let them write in their report
We are the best class they have taught!

From *Word Wizard* (OUP)

Favourite book: *Dr Xargle's Book of Earth-Hounds* by Jean Willis, illustrated by Tony Ross
Favourite colour: Turquoise
Favourite food: Chocolate mints
Favourite word: Hullabaloo
Favourite place: Honister Pass in Cumbria with its slate-grey screes and rushing streams
Where do your ideas come from? An idea may come from something that's happened to me. So I've written about giving my teddy bear a haircut and making waves in the bath. Other poems are based on observation. Then there are poems which are purely imaginary, such as 'Ten Dancing Dinosaurs' and 'The Sick Young Dragon'.
What else might you have been? For 20 years before I became a full-time writer I was an English teacher.

John Foster

Jane Gardam

I WENT TO A DREADFUL PRIVATE SCHOOL at first where we learned nothing and the headmistress was hateful towards me. Later she boasted that she had been the one to start me with books. This was not true. It all came from my mother. At the high school I was not a "good student" until I was 16. Then I suddenly began to win prizes. I also had a very good English teacher. I won a scholarship to London University and I was writing all the time and reading, reading, reading.

As a child I loved Biggles, the 'Just William' books, *Little Women*, *What Katy Did*, Beatrix Potter and Dickens. I hated Arthur Ransome. The Lake District is better than that. I wrote and acted in plays all the time with friends. I wrote poetry and loved hymns and carols. We always had a cat – he was always "mine". I had one brother who was very different and much younger, so we were never friends. My friends were books. Life would still be intolerable without them.

Date and place of birth:
11th July 1928
Coatham, Redcar,
North Yorkshire
Contact address:
Haven House
Sandwich
Kent CT13 9ES

Selected titles

The Kit Stories (Walker Books)

Bridget and William (Walker Books)

A Long Way From Verona (Abacus)

The Hollow Land (Walker Books)

Black Woolly Pony (Walker Books)

Extract

Harry looked out of the window and saw a bear, sitting on the gatepost.
It was very early in the morning and not quite light. He ran to the next bedroom where his mother and father were deep asleep with their feet sticking out here and there from the end of the bed.
"There's a bear sitting on the gatepost." Grumble, grunt.
"It has its arms stretched out."
"Go back to bed, Harry." Grumble, grunt.
"It was a bad dream."
Harry tickled the soles of some feet …

From *Tufty Bear* (Walker Books)

Favourite book: The Bible (old version)
Favourite colour: Bright orange
Favourite food: Fresh salmon fishcakes
Favourite word: Word
Favourite place: Westmorland
Where do your ideas come from? My ideas come from somewhere outside me when I am not trying to find them.

What else might you have been? Nothing; there is nothing else that I was born to do. I am glad, though, to have been a wife and mother and now a grandmother.

Jane Gardam

Alan Garner

AS SOON AS I LEARNT TO READ, in hospital at the age of 6, I read everything that was in reach. I binged on words, and still do. If I must point to one book that made all the difference to my life as a child, there are two. The first is Arthur Mee's *Children's Encyclopædia* of 1908 (in eight volumes), and the other is *The Box of Delights*, by John Masefield.

I was educated at Alderley Edge Council School, The Manchester Grammar School and Magdalen College, Oxford. I started my first novel at 16.04. on Tuesday, 4th September 1956, and have continued since. I work in front of a fire, writing in old diaries on my knee, in longhand, then revise and transfer to PC, with continuing rolling revisions of hard copy. When I'm concentrating, I am capable of trying to clean my teeth with tile cement and of putting on my glasses in order to look for them.

I like conversation, word play, laughter, the company of family and friends, being challenged to change my mind and challenging others to change theirs. I dislike, and will not tolerate, bullies; of any kind or age.

Date and place of birth:
17th October 1934
47 Crescent Road,
Congleton, Cheshire
Contact address:
Sheil Land Associates Ltd
43 Doughty Street
London WC1N 2LF
http://members.ozemail.com.
au/~xenophon/toc.html

Selected titles

The Stone Book Quartet

Elidor

The Owl Service

Red Shift

A Bag of Moonshine

All published by HarperCollins

Extract

He had not gone far when he met a thin man in the woods, and the thin man said, "Where are you going?"
"To fetch water from the springs of silver," said the boy.
"Who hates you so much," said the thin man, "that they send you there? A great cat guards the springs of silver and kills every life it sees. Did you not know? But this is the secret of the cat: when its eyes are closed, it is awake; and when its eyes are open, it is asleep."

From *The Well of the Wind* (Dorling Kindersley)

Favourites: There are so many extraordinary books, colours, foods, words, memories and places in my experience that I could not possibly set one above another.

Where do your ideas come from? I don't know where my ideas come from. It feels more that I come from the ideas. Nor do I go looking for a story. The story finds me. This may seem strange, but it is not. It is ordinary; though it is made strange by the way that many people seem to presume that writing should happen. Here's how it works. I have inside me something called an imagination, which delivers pictures, not thoughts, without my asking. I edit the pictures and stick them together, and my job is to do it so readers can experience the story that appeared to me; and then perhaps see further, by looking inside their own heads.

What else might you have been? Decomposing.

Alan Garner.

Paul Geraghty

AS A MINIATURE PERSON IN AFRICA I would spend hours in the garden and the bush watching the wildlife – from ants carrying supplies back to their nest to the Vervet monkeys and the buck that used to visit. I would imitate the birds, catch frogs and crabs in the river and draw them, and became "the class drawer" once old enough to go to school. After learning to write, I began writing stories and never stopped – not even during Maths and History. Now I write and illustrate for a living, and travel far and wide to see wildlife and the landscapes of the world.

I enjoyed books from an early age and was enchanted by Kipling's *Jungle Book* and *Just So Stories* as well as A.A. Milne's *Winnie the Pooh*.

I love music, have a massive CD collection and speakers throughout the house (which I share with a tolerant cat called Jingles!), which is almost constantly thundering with sounds (except when I write). I also play in a couple of bands and write and record music for fun.

Date and place of birth:
3rd May 1959
Durban, South Africa
Contact address:
42 Dukes Avenue
New Malden
Surrey KT3 4HN
paul.geraghty@virgin.net
http://freespace.virgin.net/
paul.geraghty/index.htm

Selected titles

Solo

The Hunter

Slobcat

The Hoppameleon

Look Out, Patrick!

All for ages 3–9, published by Hutchinson Children's Books/Red Fox

Illustration

From *The Hoppameleon* (Hutchinson Children's Books)

Favourite book: *The Church Mouse* by Graham Oakley

Favourite colour: Underwater blue

Favourite food: Avocado with salt

Favourite word: Archipelago

Favourite place: The wild coast of Africa

Where do your ideas come from? From my childhood memories. From worldwide travels (the animals and landscapes I see and photograph). From watching people, from my dreams and daydreams. From wildlife documentaries on TV and in books.

What else might you have been? A musician.

Adèle Geras

I STARTED WRITING BY ACCIDENT. I went in for a competition in the newspaper and, even though I didn't win, writing my story was such fun, I've done nothing else ever since. I've written more than 80 books for children of all ages, and I used to lie on the sofa and write in beautiful notebooks. Nowadays, though. I am a fan of the word processor and compose straight on to the computer. Magic!

We have a lovely cat called Mimi who's known as Meems. She's appeared in a lot of my stories and poems.

I am a voracious reader and a keen knitter and I love going to the movies and the theatre.

Date and place of birth:
15th March 1944
Jerusalem
Israel
Contact address:
10 Danesmoor Road
Manchester M20 3JS

Selected titles

Troy (Scholastic)

The Girls in the Velvet Frame (Collins)

The Tower Room (Red Fox)

Little Swan (Red Fox)

Wishes for You (Piccadilly Press)

Extract

"As you will see when I begin my stories, I can put down other people's innermost thoughts and feelings, conversations that have taken place miles away, and detailed descriptions of houses I never visited in the furry flesh. This is because I am a Narrator. This is a magical being who can tell you everything and take you everywhere without stirring from his cushion by the fire. In my case, it's a combination of intelligence, imagination, and a dollop of secret powers passed on to me by my Egyptian ancestors."

Ozzy, the cat who narrates the stories about the Fantora family in Book 1 of 'The Fabulous Fantoras: Book One, The Files' (Avon Books)

Favourite book: *Jane Eyre* by Charlotte Brontë
Favourite colour: Blue/green
Favourite food: Falafel in a pitta (street food in the Middle East)
Favourite word: Yesterday
Favourite place: My bed
Where do your ideas come from? My ideas come from memories of my own childhood; physical objects, such as photographs, dolls, etc.; and, most often, from places.
What else might you have been? A singer. Possibly a country-and-western singer or else a cabaret singer.

Debi Gliori

I WAS THE SAD WEE HAIRY SWOT at school – can't say I enjoyed it a whole lot …

I started growing my own family at the tender age of 17 and never looked back (5 children now). I went to Edinburgh Art College and learned how to draw. I was an only child and spent those endless summer holidays immersed in the pages of any books that came to hand, and practising being invisible while my mum and dad fell out, split up and eventually divorced. So, I guess, books were an escape and a source of comfort.

Now, in much happier times, I work in a pale grey wooden studio in my garden, drawing on a big table and writing curled up on a sofa. I feel very lucky to be able to dream for a living.

Date and place of birth:
21st February 1959
Glasgow, Scotland
Contact address:
Rosemary Sandberg
6 Bayley Street
London WC1B 3HB

Selected titles

No Matter What (Bloomsbury)

Pure Dead Magic (Doubleday)

Penguin Post (Transworld)

The Snow Lambs (Scholastic Children's Books)

Polar Bolero (David Fickling/ Scholastic)

Extract

The Tincture Topples

So close to midwinter, darkness fell at Stregaschloss around three o'clock with an almost audible thud. The wind began to gather momentum, peppering the windows with rain and causing the house's twelve chimneys to resonate in a manner that was both eerie and mournful. Clustered round an enormous log fire in the library, the clan Strega-Borgia were not inclined to be cheerful.

"I'm *freezing*," moaned Pandora for the umpteenth time.
"Put another log on then," Titus barely glanced up from his laptop.
"For heaven's sake," groaned Signora Strega-Borgia, muffled in mohair blankets, pashminas, serapes, sheepskin, slippers and woolly gloves, "we're supposed to be economising … d'you think that stuff grows on trees?"

From *Pure Dead Wicked* (Doubleday)

Favourite book: *The Little White Horse* by Elizabeth Goudge
Favourite colour: Ultramarine
Favourite food: Apple and blackcurrant crumble
Favourite word: Procrastinate
Favourite place: Loch Sween, Argyll, Scotland
Where do your ideas come from? My own childhood and the memories I have from books, films, conversations, from watching things around me with an illustrator's eye. Last but by no means least, from listening to my own children, all five of them, and remembering what it's like to be wee.
What else might you have been? I wanted to be a fairy (age 2), a princess (age 3–7), a nartist (age 7–11), a doctor (age 13–15), an astrophysicist (age 16–18), an artist (age 19), a writer (age 20–42).

Pippa Goodhart

I WAS BROUGHT UP IN A VILLAGE and went to the village school where there were two classes, infants and juniors. It came as a shock when I had to go to a secondary school with over a thousand children in it! I think that I am different from most writers in that I didn't always long to be an author. I was very slow at learning to read and never very neat at writing. I still can't spell. But I was good at playing imaginary games when I was a child, and perhaps that was my practice for making up stories. I had a brother and a sister and a best friend next door to play with, so I was lucky. And I used to imagine myself being a part of the stories that I read in books.

I trained to be a teacher, but couldn't get a teaching job, so I went back to the bookshop where I had a Saturday job while still at school. They put me in the children's bookshop. I stayed for five years, ending up as the manager with the big key that opened the dungeon downstairs (honest!). In those years I met authors and publishers and read and read and read. I learned a lot. But I didn't begin writing until later when I was at home being a mum. And now I can't stop. I love it! I live with my husband and three daughters, a cat and a dog, and I've got the best job in the world. Lucky me!

Date and place of birth:
27th September 1958
Cambridge
Contact address:
Egmont Children's Books
239 Kensington High Street
London W8 6SL

Selected titles

Row Your Boat – picture book (Mammoth)

Flow (Mammoth)

Happy Sad (Mammoth)

Alona's Story (Mammoth)

Molly and the Beanstalk (Walker Books)

Extract

Ginny watched as the little creature slowly uncurled and revealed itself, pulling itself free of the sticky egginess that had stuck it down in an oval huddle and dulled the colours of its body. She watched as the head and neck uncurled. The head had large nostrils and surprising lines of dark lashes on either side marking where the eyes were. But the eyes themselves stayed closed. As the unseeing head rose on its long neck, the little body lurched back, and wobbly short scaly legs uncurled and propped up its front half. Another lurch and the back legs were up and a miniature dragon stood for a moment before it crumpled down again onto the sheet. Two more faltering tries, and then he stood firm.
"Hello, Egg," whispered Ginny.

From *Ginny's Egg* (Mammoth)

Favourite book: *Dogger* by Shirley Hughes
Favourite colour: Blue
Favourite food: Fresh scones, cream and strawberry jam
Favourite word: Snert
Favourite place: Sitting in bed watching my three little daughters performing a special Easter show they had secretly prepared for their dad and me.
Where do your ideas come from? Most of my ideas come from looking at the people and the world around me and wondering "what if …?" I get to know my characters, then I put them into an interesting situation and see how they react. I like to try things out in stories that I would never or could never do in real life – like magic, for instance! I'm not a great planner of stories.
What else might you have been? I trained to be a teacher, but I go into schools now and realise that I've got the easier job! Perhaps I could have been a publisher and asked all my favourite authors to write stories for me to publish!

Pippa Goodhart

Mick Gowar

PHOTO: ALEXANDRA BURKE

I DIDN'T LIKE BEING AT SCHOOL. Most of the time seemed to be spent learning lists of dates, verbs and capital cities for tests and exams, and being shouted at – and occasionally hit – by the teachers (this was in the 1960s). But I did like some of things that went on in school – writing poems and stories, drawing and acting in the school plays.

After I left college, I worked as a journalist on a financial paper and then writing press releases in a PR company. I always knew I wanted to write stories and poems, but I didn't know who I wanted to write for or what I wanted to write about. It was Ruth Craft, who wrote *The Winter Bear* and the 'Fancy Nancy' stories, who suggested I try writing for children. As soon as I started my first children's poems I knew that writing for children was what I had to do.

I like to write a mixture of poems, stories, and non-fiction books rather than specialising in one type of writing. I also really enjoy working with artists from other disciplines – musicians, visual artists, dancers – on educational projects to help children and adults to explore lots of different ways to express their ideas and feelings.

Date and place of birth:
27th November 1951
Harrow, Middlesex
Contact address:
12 Quainton Close
Cambridge CB5 8LR
mick.gowar1@ntlworld.com

Selected titles

Yallery Brown – retelling of traditional Suffolk story, based on children's opera written with the composer Glyn Evans (Scholastic Hippo)

Arthur: Warrior Chief – new versions of Arthurian stories (OUP)

Carnival of the Animals – poetry collection for 8–13 years (Puffin)

Marie-Antoinette – historical biography for 10–14 years (Miles Kelly Publishing)

Caroline Columbus – short stories for 5–8 years (Walker Books)

Extract

It's chilly on the touch line, but
with all my kit on
underneath my clothes
I'm not too cold. Besides,
I've got a job to do:
    I'm Third Reserve
    I run the line.
I've been the Third Reserve all season,
every Saturday.
I've never missed a match:
At home, Away
it's all the same to me
    'Cos I'm the Third Reserve,
    The bloke who runs the line.

From *Third Time Lucky* (Puffin)

Favourite books: *Nothing to be Afraid Of* by Jan Mark; *Beowulf* – especially Seamus Heaney's translation

Favourite colour: Blue

Favourite food: Mussels and chips – as served in Belgium

Favourite word: Lunch

Favourite place: Visiting Toronto with my daughter about ten years ago. We had a wonderful time, and I felt instantly at home in Canada. I'd love to go back and stay for at least a couple of months, but so far I've either been too busy or too broke to do it.

Where do your ideas come from? I get ideas from stories and poems I've read, music I've listened to and pictures and films I've seen.

What else might you have been? I would probably have been a frustrated writer. I expect I would have ended up teaching full-time, but wishing I could write instead.

Mick Gowar.

Michael Hardcastle

SPORT HAS ALWAYS BEEN A PASSION since my schooldays, mainly because I hardly played any then. Because of a succession of illnesses, ranging from diphtheria to rheumatic fever, I was sent to the library during games periods to read anything of my choice. I didn't mind that too much because I discovered the joy of fiction while in hospital or recuperating at home. But what the library shelves lacked was any stories about football or cricket or horse-racing, let alone the less popular sports. Which is why, after I'd proved my fitness by joining the army at 18 and then working on a daily newspaper, I started to write sports fiction – and found that I had a field practically to myself.

I visit a lot of schools during a year and I particularly enjoy those possessing table-tennis equipment who invite me to have a game with a pupil or teacher at some stage. That was the only game I played regularly at school and we used the tables of the biology lab which were very long and had gas taps fitted at intervals. I learned that if you served so that the ball struck the tap in your opponent's half he had no chance at all of winning that point. So, sometimes, you see, I did enjoy sport at school.

Date and place of birth:
6th February in a year Everton won the FA Cup Huddersfield, West Yorkshire
Contact address:
17 Molescroft Park
Beverley
Yorkshire HU17 7EB
Tel/fax 01482 868350

Selected titles

Quake – a novel about family relationships (Faber)

Walking the Goldfish – a Banana Book (Heinemann)

Carole's Camel (Heinemann)

The Most Dangerous Score – in my 'Goal Kings' series (Faber)

Please Come Home (Faber)

Extract

Now there was pandemonium. The yells had turned into screams of terror and the quaking beneath their feet continued. The first roof tiles crashed through the glass dome and shards of glass fell like lethal hailstones. As Caroline somehow managed to stay upright she saw a wall coming towards her: and it wasn't an optical illusion. The buildings around her were dancing a devilish jig, putting on a crazy rock 'n' roll exhibition.

Now, with a desperate effort, she managed to reach a doorway. But the remorseless terrifying shaking of the ground prevented her from going anywhere else. She clutched at the door-frame for support. Then, in rising horror, she saw what was happening to the people who hadn't been able to move from the centre of the bombarded arcade.

From *Quake* (Faber)

Favourite book: *Great Expectations* by Charles Dickens
Favourite colour: Green
Favourite food: Smoked salmon
Favourite word: Bizarre
Favourite place: Switzerland
Where do your ideas come from? Most of my ideas originate as a result of personal observation, or from anecdotes that people tell me, and that's why I always carry a pocket notebook wherever I go.
What else might you have been? I would have been happy to continue as a journalist because I revelled in the excitement of life on a daily newspaper.

Michael Harrison

I THINK THE MAJOR INFLUENCE ON MY WRITING has been Enid Blyton. I loved her books when I was a child, especially the 'Adventure' series, and would lose myself totally in them. When I became a teacher of English I realised how badly written and shallow they were. I looked for books of real quality that gave the same intensity of grip, but found very few. I started to write one myself but I couldn't do it because my own children were the same age as the heroes of the story and I thought that if I put my characters into real danger something awful might happen to my children too. The book turned into a comedy, *Bags of Trouble*, and had two sequels, the second of which, *Trouble in Store*, is very much a story about writing stories in school. When my children were grown up I tried again and did manage to frighten myself, which is perhaps the real test, with *It's My Life*.

Date and place of birth:
7th June 1939
Oxford
Contact address:
Mjacharrison@aol.com

Selected titles

Junk Mail – my poems for children

It's My Life – thriller, 9–14 years

Facing the Dark – thriller, 9–14 years

At the Deep End – thriller, 9–14 years

Don Quixote: a Retelling

All published by OUP

Extract

Dad was arrested for murder on Tuesday. When the door closed behind the police Mum and I just sat on the sofa and stared at the floor for what seemed a very long time. Then she went out across the hall to the kitchen and I heard her filling the kettle. She brought me a mug of very sweet tea and told me to drink it. She sounded strange, as if she was a very long way away, or perhaps I was. Everything had changed the moment I opened the door to the two men. It was worse, somehow, that I had been the one to let them in, the one who ended our family life. It had been very quick: Is your father in? I'm Inspector Something and this is Sergeant Something Else. Could we have a word with him, please? And then reciting his rights to him, so familiar from watching *The Bill*. And they were gone and we were left.
"What's he done?" I said, staring into my mug of tea.
"Nothing," Mum said. "It's a mistake, you'll see."

From *Facing the Dark* (OUP)

Favourite book: *The Mouse and his Child* by Russell Hoban
Favourite colour: Blue
Favourite food: Any fish except plaice
Favourite word: Serendipity – both for its sound and because it is the most important way to learn.
Favourite memory: Walking in Italy.
Where do your ideas come from? For me walking is the best way of preparing to write, in France or Italy for choice, but the truth is that the only way to write is just to sit down and write. I am quite disciplined. I shut myself in my writing room every morning and don't come out until I have written at least 500 words. I get the beginning of a story quite clearly in my mind but I never plan the book at all. I write the story because I want to find out what happens. All my best ideas come while I am actually writing.

Michael Harrison

Anne Harvey

I WAS A READING AND WRITING CHILD, called the Bookworm. I grew up in World War 2 and remember air raids, drinking hot cocoa, singing songs and playing games. We children put on concerts to cheer people up. My grandmother recited poems to us and my grandfather was a music-hall comedian, so performing and learning by heart became second nature to me.

At school I enjoyed English, history, French, drama and art. My best friend Ann and I organised the class plays and edited a magazine called *The Anapœst*. She grew up to be a well-known children's writer and a biographer and we're still friends.

I began making anthologies of my favourite poems when I was about 12 and have never stopped. My favourite books, which I still love, were *The Swish of the Curtain* by Pamela Brown and *Ballet Shoes* by Noel Streatfeild. After drama school training I ran my own theatre in Cornwall for three years. Other influences are Walter de la Mare and Eleanor Farjeon. They both knew that children can listen to, appreciate and read fine writing, not only what is easy and recognisable.

Date and place of birth:
27th April 1933
London
Contact address:
37 St Stephen's Road
Ealing
London W13 8HJ
0208 997 6443

Selected titles

Swings and Shadows (Red Fox)

Shades of Green (Red Fox)

Adlestrop Revisited (Sutton Publishing)

The Naughtiest Children I Know (Red Fox)

In Time of War (Macmillan Children's Books)

Extract

Stage Fright

The audience is good. A lucky sign.
Yet I am frightened and my heart beats fast.
I've felt like this so many times before
While waiting in the wings with all the cast.
They're talking gaily. Don't they feel the same?
Why can't they feel the tension in the air?
Oh, dear, I want to blow my nose again –
I've smudged my lipstick! Quick! – A glass! My hair!
I simply can't go on. Why do I feel
As though my heart will leave my body soon?
Too late to find an understudy now –
The orchestra is playing the last tune.
What's my first line? You're sure? There is no doubt?
I'm on! "Er ... Sire, your carriage is without."

From Queen Elizabeth's Girls Grammar School magazine 1947, written at age 14

Favourite book: *A Nursery in the Nineties* by Eleanor Farjeon
Favourite colour: Purple
Favourite food: Eggs
Favourite word: Shadow or swing
Favourite memory: Discovering Shakespeare
Where do your ideas come from? From my childhood, family, friends and school; from books I've read and plays I've seen; from my growing-up time, relationships, children and grand-children (Amelia and Edmund); all that has happened – all these are influences that clamour to be remembered, recreated or reinvented.

What else might you have been? I was an actor and would have continued in the theatre, had I not had children, taught drama and begun writing and editing books. I might have managed a bookshop or worked as a librarian ... any job with books. I still do a great deal of performing and poetry reading on stage and radio.

Anne Harvey

Jane Hissey

AS A CHILD I WAS ALWAYS READING, writing or drawing. I read anything exciting, I drew everything and I wrote stories and terrible poems (which I thought were quite good at the time!). I went on to train as an illustrator, then to teach art and, finally, I began writing and illustrating my own books! *Old Bear* was the first. Since then I have produced about a book a year and 40 episodes of *Old Bear Stories* for TV.

I use coloured pencils to do my drawings and I have all the real toys sitting in front of me when I am drawing them (or writing about them). As well as a house full of old toys, there are five of us – me, my husband Ivan (who is also an illustrator) and our children Owen, Alison and Ralph. We have one cat, two chickens and countless goldfish in the pond. I'm never bored.

Date and place of birth:
1st September 1952,
Norwich, Norfolk
Contact address:
Random House
61–63 Uxbridge Road
London W5 5SA

Selected titles

Old Bear (Red Fox)

Little Bear's Trousers (Red Fox)

Ruff (Red Fox)

Little Bear's Dragon (Red Fox)

Old Bear's All-together Painting (Hutchinson Children's Books)

Illustration

From *Old Bear's All-together Painting* (Hutchinson Children's Books)

Favourite book: *Dogger* by Shirley Hughes (I wish I'd written it!)

Favourite colour: Brown

Favourite food: Home-made bread with sunflower seeds

Favourite word: Holiday

Favourite memory: Sitting reading in my grandmother's old apple tree – all day!

Where do your ideas come from? I write lists of things I would like to draw and incorporate in my stories! I also watch children playing and try to remember the games that I used to play with my toys when I was little. And my own children help me with ideas when I'm stuck.

What else might you have been? I almost trained as a sculptor because I love modelling and carving. Later on I nearly trained as a medical illustrator because I liked the idea of combining science and art! But now I love gardening and when I am not at my drawing board or writing I'm out in my garden planting, weeding or mowing the grass. So perhaps I would have been a garden designer if I hadn't become an author and illustrator.

Jane Hissey

Anthony Horowitz

AT THE AGE OF 8 I WAS SENT TO ORLEY FARM, a really foul boarding school in north London. The teachers were extremely cruel. Some of them had even won prizes for cruelty. But one thing I do have to thank the place for is that it encouraged me to write. I began telling stories and writing as a means of escape. At the same time, I loved reading. I read the Narnia books, Tintin and all the 'Adventures' by Willard Price.

I still live in north London but now with an amusing wife, two children and a dog called Lucky (who isn't – he's been run over three times, once by me). I spend most of my time writing … not just children's books but TV scripts and horror films. My greatest fear is that I'll drop dead when I'm half-way through a new book.

Date and place of birth:
5th April 1955
London
Contact address:
ajhorowitz@aol.com

Selected titles

Stormbreaker – the first Alex Rider book (Walker Books)

Point Blanc – sequel to *Stormbreaker* (Walker Books)

Horowitz Horror – a collection of really scary horror stories (Orchard Books)

Granny (Walker Books)

The Falcon's Malteser – the first story of the Diamond brothers (Walker Books)

Extract

I like horror stories – but not when they happen to me. If you've read my other adventures, you'll know that I've been smothered in concrete, locked up with a dangerous lunatic, tied to a railway line, almost blown up, chased through a cornfield dodging machine gun bullets, poisoned in Paris … and all this before my fourteenth birthday. It's not fair. I do my homework. I clean my teeth twice a day. Why does everyone want to kill me?

But the worst thing that ever happened to me began on a hot morning in July. The summer holidays had just begun and I was looking forward to eight weeks with my big brother, Tim, the world's most unsuccessful private detective. Tim had just spent a month helping with security at the American Embassy in Grosvenor Square and even now I'm not sure how he'd decided there was a bomb in the ambassador's car. Anyway, just as the ambassador was about to get in, Tim grabbed hold of him and hurled him out of the way which would have been heroic if there had been a bomb (there wasn't) and if Tim hadn't managed to throw the unfortunate man in front of a passing bus. The ambassador was now in hospital. And Tim, as usual, was out of work.

From *I Know What You Did Last Wednesday* (Walker Books)

Favourite books: *Bleak House* by Charles Dickens (adult); *I am the Cheese* by Robert Cormier (kid)
Favourite colour: Royal blue (ink)
Favourite food: Boiled egg
Favourite word: Muesli (as in "We are not a muesli")
Favourite place: Orford, Suffolk. It's where I go to write.
Where do your ideas come from? My ideas come from newspaper stories, snippets of conversation and by constantly asking "What if…?" These are two of my favourite words. I also love day-dreaming. I have about a hundred ideas a day… though not many of them are any good.
What else might you have been? The sad truth is that writing is the only thing that I'm any good at and if I wasn't a writer I suppose I would have to sell parts of myself for experiments or perhaps become a traffic warden. I am very lucky to earn a living out of something I love doing.

Lesley Howarth

I STARTED WRITING POEMS AND STORIES from about the age of 7. At 11, I produced a magazine called *Lesley's Gazette* and sold it at school! Later, I loved reading many different kinds of books, particularly science fiction, poetry, the 'Just William' books, H.G. Wells; an early influence was Grimms' *Fairy Tales* – the illustrations from that book are imprinted on my brain!

Our family has a cat called Maisie. She loves to walk over my work in the office!

Date and place of birth:
29th December 1952
Bournemouth
Contact address:
Puffin Books
80 Strand
London WC2R 0RL

Selected titles

Ultraviolet (Puffin)

Carwash (Puffin)

MapHead (Walker Books)

Paulina (Walker Books)

Mister Spaceman (Walker Books)

Extract

Imagine you never went to school. Never went out with your friends. Stayed home and studied on the computer. Not now and then. All the time. You have a best friend named Reeve. You see her whenever you can. Other friends, maybe you email or "meet" in guestrooms in games like The Quest. A night out? Forget it. Everyone forgot how to "do" friends, now no one goes out any more.

From *Ultraviolet* (Puffin)

Favourite book: *Kidnapped* by R.L. Stevenson
Favourite colour: Green
Favourite food: Greek yoghurt
Favourite word: Mellifluous
Where do your ideas come from? My surroundings, friends and family, and daily events that crop up are all sources for my ideas.
What else might you have been? A gardener

Lesley Howarth

Janni Howker

I AM OFTEN ASKED WHEN I STARTED WRITING and the answer is that I was about 4½ to 5 years old, like most children.

The truth is that I never stopped.

Most young children write, paint, play, sing, make things, dance, run, jump, climb trees etc. etc. Sadly, by the time most young people leave school they have stopped doing many things that used to help them explore the world imaginatively.

Date and place of birth:
6th July 1957
Nicosia, Cyprus
Contact address:
The Cottage
Cumwhitton
Brampton
Cumbria CA8 9EX

Selected titles

Walk with the Wolf – picture book (Walker Books)

Badger on the Barge – short stories, 9–14 (Walker Books)

Isaac Campion – 12+ (Walker Books)

The Nature of the Beast – 10+ (Walker Books)

Martin Farrell – 12+ (Red Fox)

Extract

Howl with a wolf in the dawn, thin and icy. Deep from her chest the eerie sound comes.

Long, low music. The song of the Arctic.

Another howl answers.

With a wag of her tail, the wolf runs to the pack. Three sons and a daughter, cubs from the spring, squirm on their bellies and lick at her neck.

The black wolf greets her with a stare from his pale eyes. He's her mate, the pack's strongest hunter – and he's hungry too.

From *Walk with the Wolf* (Walker Books)

Favourite book: *What is the Truth?* by Ted Hughes
Favourite colour: Gold
Favourite food: Lamb chops, new potatoes, carrots and peas!
Favourite place: Watching basking sharks off Argyll.
Where do your ideas come from? Ideas come from the application of imagination to experience. It's the same application which makes some people artists and some people worriers. If I hear a strange noise in the middle of the night I might get an idea for a story or worry that a bear is in the corridor – a hungry bear with big teeth …
What else might you have been? I am a mother as well as a writer and I also like fishing and cooking. I studied archaeology for a time but as a child I wanted to be an explorer and naturalist … I think what drives me is curiosity. Whatever I did I would be curious!

Janni Howker

46

Roderick Hunt

BEFORE I BEGIN WRITING I sit quietly and try to "see" the story in my mind's eye – just like I would if I were watching a TV screen. I've always done that. It's almost like day dreaming, and it got me into trouble at school because the teachers thought I'd gone to sleep, or wasn't paying attention. As a child I loved reading and even when I read a book that had no pictures at all, I could see pictures in my imagination just like looking at a film. My favourite books were adventure stories and I loved *Treasure Island* by R.L. Stevenson.

I enjoyed telling stories to my sons John and David when they were little. One night we had some friends staying so there were five children in the house. At bedtime a tray of hot drinks was spilled all over the carpet. Disaster! Children were crying; grown-ups were shouting. So I sat all the children on the sofa and made up a story to tell them. My story-telling was so successful I had to do it every bedtime for three nights. Later I wrote the stories down, and they were the first ones I had published.

Date and place of birth:
7th June 1939
Marlborough, Wiltshire
Contact address:
Brooklyn
Wilsham Road, Abingdon
Oxfordshire OX14 5HP
rodwrite@aol.com
www.oup.co.uk/primary

Selected titles

The Oxford Reading Tree – over 250 stories

Oxford Reading Tree Rhyme and Analogy, 12 titles

Wolf Hill – 30 titles

Ghosts, Witches and Things Like That

The Magic Key – TV series, tie-in story books

All published by OUP

Extract

Suddenly the magic key began to glow.
The magic took the children off on another adventure.
From *What Was It Like?*, illustrated by Alex Brychta (OUP)

Favourite book: *Captain Corelli's Mandolin* by Louis de Bernières
Favourite colour: Blue
Favourite food: Fruit
Favourite word: Varmint
Favourite place: Crooks Peak in Somerset.
Where do your ideas come from? Because I write so many little stories I'm always looking out for something that will trigger an idea for a story. For example, I once saw some children giving each other rides in an old armchair someone had dumped on the street. The chair had big castors so it was like a giant skateboard.
What else might you have been? I was a teacher for 20 years and that's what I would still have been if I hadn't given up to be a writer. Teaching is a great job and I love it.

Roderick Hunt

Pat Hutchins

MY PRIMARY SCHOOL was in a small village surrounded by countryside, and I would have much rather been exploring the countryside than sitting in a classroom. I had four brothers, a sister, and a pet crow called Sooty. My most treasured possession, apart from Sooty, was a proper, spiral-bound sketchbook that my mum had bought me because I loved drawing. Sooty was too lazy to fly, so with him perched on my shoulder we would set off across the fields, and while I stopped to sketch, he would search for grubs to eat, although his favourite food was ice-cream.

I loved writing as well as drawing, and I would force my family to sit down and listen to my stories. I wrote songs, too, which they refused to sit down and listen to, as I wasn't very good at singing. Reading was another passion. *The Arabian Nights* was my all-time favourite, closely followed by *The Secret Garden* and *Girls' Crystal* magazine.

When I had children of my own, it was wonderful to sit them down and read them published stories I'd written. But even they refused to sit down and listen to my songs – I'm afraid that my voice never improved.

Date and place of birth:
18th June 1942
Catterick Camp
North Yorkshire
Contact address:
75 Flask Walk
London NW3 1ET
www.titch.net

Selected titles

Rosie's Walk

Titch

Don't Forget the Bacon

Ten Red Apples

The House that Sailed Away

All published by Red Fox

Illustration

From *Three Star Billy* (Red Fox)

Favourite book: *The Arabian Nights*
Favourite colour: Cornflower blue
Favourite food: Pease pudding
Favourite word: Sympathy
Favourite place: My cottage garden in June
Where do your ideas come from? My ideas come from looking and listening, and occasionally eavesdropping! The idea for *The Very Worst Monster* came from my niece, Amy, when she was 3. Amy's mum was expecting another baby, and when I asked Amy what she was going to do with the new baby when it arrived, she said "Give it away." So I wrote a story about a monster who gives her baby brother away.

What else might you have been? A singer or dancer, but as I can't sing or dance, I would have tried to work as a theatre designer. But I still like writing best!

Pat Hutchins

Rose Impey

WHEN I WAS 7 and just getting started as an independent reader, my mum had a baby. I already had two sisters. Suddenly our little house seemed too full. I had to share a bedroom – a bed, even – with my younger sister! There was literally nowhere to be on my own.

So I would sneak out, onto the back step and read for hours. My bottom might have been on the step but my head was off travelling with the Famous Five to Smugglers Top, or with Heidi up a mountain, or with Jim Hawkins bound for Treasure Island. That was the beginning for me. Of course, it was many years before I thought of becoming a writer. I was a teacher first. I spent hours reading to classes, rediscovering the power of stories. Slowly I realised I wanted to write my own.

Now, when I write, I have a sense of that original class inside my head, which is why it matters to me that my work should read aloud well. I read everything out loud, over and over, which is why I like to work in an empty house. What a luxury that seems now.

Date and place of birth:
7th June 1947
Northwich, Cheshire
Contact address:
Orchard Books
96 Leonard Street
London EC2A 4XD

Selected titles

A Letter to Father Christmas – picture book (Orchard Books)

Fireballs from Hell – 9–11 years (HarperCollins)

The Flat Man (HarperCollins)

Animal Crackers – series for 5–8 years (Orchard Books)

Desperate for a Dog – in 'Jets' series for 6–8 years (HarperCollins)

Extract

At night when it is dark
and I am in bed
and I can't get to sleep
I hear noises.
I hear tap, tap, tap.
I know what it is.
It's a tree blowing in the wind.
It taps on the glass. That's all.
But I like to pretend
it's The Flat Man trying to get in.
His long, bony fingers tap on the glass.
"Let me in," he whispers.
Tap, tap, tap.
I like scaring myself.
It's only a game.

From *The Flat Man* (Mathew Price Ltd)

Favourite book: *The Eighteenth Emergency* by Betsy Byars
Favourite colour: Blue
Favourite food: Exotic fruit salad
Favourite word: Veracity
Favourite place: Hard to choose between Edinburgh – I love the dramatic skyline – and Sydney – likewise. Although they couldn't be more different.

Where do your ideas come from? Sometimes they appear like little gifts, from things other people say or do. Other times, in quiet moments, they bubble to the surface from who knows where. Both feel like magic.
What else might you have been? I was a teacher for a while, so I'd probably be teaching – and heading for a nervous breakdown.

Curtis Jobling

Date and place of birth:
14th February 1972
Blackpool
Contact address:
Laura Cecil Agency
17 Alwyne Villas
London N1 2HG

I WAS A SMALL, SOME WOULD SAY GINGER, CHILD at school. The only reason I wasn't picked on by anyone was that my next-door neighbour was the school bully, and in return for protection I would dance like a monkey for his amusement. Mum says I was never happier than when I had a crayon in my hand. That as well as a chocolate bar.

I do most of my work from home, where my studio is set up to my liking. To the untrained eye it would look like a pigsty, but there is method in my madness. Honest.

I also work in the week on "Bob the Builder", which I designed. My favourite books as a child were *Dr Seuss*, *Where the Wild Things Are* and, most influentially, *The Hobbit*.

All of the above is true, Cub Scout's honour, except the monkey dance thing …

Illustration

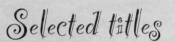

From *Frankenstein's Cat* (Hodder Children's Books)

Selected titles

Frankenstein's Cat (Hodder Children's Books)

Dinosaurs after Dark (HarperCollins)

Favourite book: *The Hobbit* by J.R.R. Tolkien
Favourite colour: Blue
Favourite food: Fajitas (homemade, naturally)
Favourite word: Hapless
Favourite place: Tuscany
Where do your ideas come from? Anywhere and everywhere. I've always been a bit of a daydreamer so ideas can strike at the oddest of times. I conceived *Frankenstein's Cat* on a crowded train journey down to London, scribbling the words and drawing a thumbnail picture with a wobbly hand in my pocket sketchbook.
What else might you have been? I always wanted to be an archaeologist à la Indiana Jones. That or a lumberjack …

Terry Jones

I ALWAYS WANTED TO BE A WRITER. I remember writing poems and things around the age of 7. I knew then I didn't want to stop. I wrote "I'm hopping to be an actor" – well, I'm still hopping. But I knew deep down that it was writing I loved.

My grammar school seemed to drain that ambition out of me – it began to seem impossible even to consider a career in writing, and I somehow got reconciled to the idea that the nearest would be to become a teacher or university researcher. It was in my final year at Oxford, sitting in the Bodleian Library, writing about what somebody else had written about what somebody else had written about Milton or someone that I realised that I wanted to write the stuff that was being written about rather than writing about other people's writing.

So when I left university I thought – I've got to try and do what I've always wanted to do. It didn't matter what – I just wanted to write. TV seemed the most likely place to start. So that's what I did – writing and performing comedy for TV and cinema.

Writing my books of stories came later, when my daughter Sally was 5. I thought: "Great! I can read her some fairy tales," but when I started reading the Brothers Grimm I thought … they really are a bit grim and I decided I'd have a go at writing stories myself. That's how I started.

Date and place of birth:
1st February 1942, Colwyn Bay, North Wales
Contact address:
34 Thistlewaite Road
London E5 0QQ
feggfeat@macline.co.uk

Selected titles

Fairy Tales and Fantastic Stories (Pavilion)

Nicobobinus (Puffin)

Erik the Viking (Robson Books)

The Curse of the Vampire's Socks (Pavilion)

The Knight and the Squire/The Lady and the Squire (Puffin)

Extract

Mouldy Land

In Mouldy Land
In Mouldy Land
They buy their mice in tins.
They race elastic bandages,
And shoot whoever wins.

The shops are full of cobweb pies.
The buses have bad feet.
They've Homes For Eaten Sandwiches,
Dead-ends to every street.

And yet the people there live well
– As far as they can see –
As long as they've got treacle farts
And buttered bums for tea.

From *The Curse of the Vampire's Socks* (Pavilion)

Favourite book: *Northern Lights* by Philip Pullman
Favourite colour: Green
Favourite food: Everything edible
Favourite word: Edible
Favourite place: Wales
Where do your ideas come from? My ideas simply come from thin air.

What else might you have been? I'd probably have been a film director … but, wait a minute, I sometimes am! Well, in that case I'd write about Geoffrey Chaucer.

Terry Jones

Ann Jungman

I WOULD LOVE TO BE ABLE TO TELL you that I was tall and thin and amazingly beautiful but, alas, that is not the case. The reality is a short, dark, rather plump woman.

My parents came from Germany as refugees from Hitler. During the War I was evacuated to Usk in Wales, a beautiful place; the rest of the time I was in London. The only school subjects I was any good at were English and history. I also liked acting and making up plays. After leaving school I got a law degree and became a barrister. Then I decided I'd rather teach. As a teacher I was always telling stories to my class. They thought I should write them down and I did.

Years ago I went to live in Australia with my husband. Now I live in London again, spending about three months a year Down Under.

Apart from writing and visiting schools, I run a small publishing company called Barn Owl Books, and I have loads of fun reprinting children's books. Look out for Barn Owl Books in your libraries and bookshops. And if you have a favourite book you can't get hold of, write and tell me.

Date and place of birth:
19th December 1938
London
Contact address:
157 Fortis Green Road
London N110 3HX
ann.jungmann@pop3.poptel.
org.uk

Selected titles

Romans: *Clottus and the Ghostly Gladiator* – 7–9 years (A & C Black)

Sasha and the Wolfcub – 6–9 years (Collins)

Dragon Disasters – 6–9 years (Scholastic)

Lucy and the Big Bad Wolf – 8–12 years (Collins)

Cinderella and the Hot Air Balloon – picture book, 5–7 years (Frances Lincoln)

Extract

Clottus and Twitta are watching a gladiatorial match with their parents.

The winner put his foot on the armoured gladiator's chest and drew his sword. He turned to the spectators.
"Kill him, kill him!" chanted the crowd and turned their thumbs down.
"Spare him, spare him!" shouted Clottus and Twitta, who felt sorry for the fallen gladiator. Everyone looked at the governor. His decision was the only one that mattered.
Suddenly Clottus noticed that the fallen gladiator had a mark on his leg sticking out below the armour, a familiar mark!

From Romans: *Clottus and the Ghostly Gladiator* (A & C Black)

Favourite book: *Huckleberry Finn* by Mark Twain
Favourite colour: Grey
Favourite food: Pancakes
Favourite word: Perambulate
Favourite place: Kangaroo Valley in New South Wales, Australia
Where do your ideas come from? Whenever something unusual happens I remember it and try to turn it into a story. One time I was visiting a school and a fire broke out. I decided it was a dragon who caused it. So far I have written two successful books about that dragon! I always worry that I have had my very last idea but then I read something, or see something, or experience something and there is a lovely new idea.

What else might you have been? A director in the theatre or a picture researcher or on the news at the BBC.

Jackie Kay

I WAS ADOPTED AND BROUGHT UP IN GLASGOW. I started writing at 12. I always liked keeping my own notebooks and writing poems or stories outside of school work.

I had an imaginary dog called Bongo. I had a real rabbit called Harvey, a guinea-pig called Shandy, and two gerbils called Eric and Ernie after the comedians Morecambe and Wise. There were also two budgies – Paddy and Yuri (after Yuri Gagarin).

I work in my attic and when I travel – on trains. I loved *Anne of Green Gables* as a child. I called my son Matthew after Matthew in that book because he was kind. I had an imaginary friend called Brendon Gallacher.

Date and place of birth:
9th November 1961
Scotland
Contact address:
25 Macefin Avenue
Manchester
M21 7QQ
jackie.kay@btinternet.com

Selected titles

Two's Company (Puffin)

The Frog who Dreamed She Was an Opera Singer (Bloomsbury)

Read Me – edited by Gaby Morgan (Macmillan Children's Books)

Strawgirl (Macmillan)

Five Finger-Piglets (Macmillan Children's Books)

Extract

He was seven and I was six, my Brendon Gallacher.
He was Irish and I was Scottish, my Brendon Gallacher.
His father was in prison; he was a cat burglar.
My father was a communist party full-time worker.
He had six brothers and I had one, my Brendon Gallacher.

He would hold my hand and take me by the river
where we'd talk all about his family being poor.
He'd get his mum out of Glasgow when he got older.
A wee holiday some place nice. Same place far.
I'd tell my mum about my Brendon Gallacher.

How his mum drank and his daddy was a cat burglar.
And she'd say, "why not have him round to dinner?"
No, no, I'd say, he's got big holes in his trousers.
I like meeting him by the burn in the open air.

From 'Brendon Gallacher', *Two's Company* (Puffin)

Favourite book: *Middlemarch* by George Eliot
Favourite colour: Turquoise
Favourite food: Cous-cous, curry
Favourite word: Serendipity
Favourite place: Isle of Mull, Scotland
Where do your ideas come from? People mainly – how people talk. People and landscape and music and imagination. I like writing that is a mixture of real-life experience and imagination, the familiar and strange. I like making things up, mixing true and false.
What else might you have been? An actress. I always wanted to act and when I was a child I went to the Royal Scottish Academy of Music and Drama. I liked the idea of pretending to be somebody else – but you get to do that when you write anyway!

Dick King-Smith

I WAS AT BOARDING SCHOOLS in the 1930s. I didn't try writing a book for children till I was in my 50s. I work in a very small study in my very old cottage. I have 13 grandchildren and 2 great-granddaughters, the produce of my own son and 2 daughters. Over the years I have had hundreds of pets; now only seven chickens. I like reading, sitting in my garden, washing up, most TV nature programmes, and especially, the masses of letters I get from children all over the world. I dislike cruelty to animals (or people), loud music from trannies, anyone who chucks rubbish about in the countryside, nuts, pineapples and turnips. I am frightened of travelling in aeroplanes (so I don't). When I take off my shoes, I always put them neatly side by side and when I see a magpie, I bow and say "Good morning, my lord."

The books I enjoyed as a child include all Beatrix Potter, most A.A. Milne and a lot of Kipling. Then there were *The Wind in the Willows* and nature books by Ernest Thompson Seton and Charles G.D. Roberts.

Date and place of birth:
27th March 1922
Bitton, Gloucestershire
Contact address:
Penguin UK
80 Strand
London WC2R 0RL

Selected titles

The Sheep-Pig (Puffin)

The Hodgeheg (Puffin)

The Roundhill (Puffin)

The Crowstarver (Corgi)

Lady Daisy (Puffin)

Extract

Splat!

No creature can create it
Or hope to imitate it.
To do this thing no other beast knows how.

However much they practise,
The plain and simple fact is –
No-one can make a cowpat like a cow.

From *Jungle Jingles* – book of verse (Doubleday)

Favourite book: *The Jungle Book* by Rudyard Kipling
Favourite colour: No favourite – I like lots
Favourite food: Fish pie with an eggy sauce
Favourite word: Home
Favourite place: My garden
Where do your ideas come from? Things I've done – people I've met – animals I've known – places that are important; all these are sources of my ideas.

Quite a lot of my tales are really love stories, sometimes about toads or beetles or woodlice, or people.
What else might you have been? I am a failed farmer. It would have been nice to be a successful one, but I'm very happy just writing.

Dick King-Smith

Robert Leeson

MY FIRST STORIES were told in the playground at primary school, sometimes dreams I remembered, sometimes tales I'd read and re-told, with me in the action. In secondary school I wrote short stories instead of homework essays. Instead of telling me off, the English teacher encouraged me. My mother got me a library ticket. The librarian gave me free run of the shelves; *Treasure Island* and *The House at Pooh Corner* were two favourites.

Today, after nearly 30 years' travelling, I've retired from visiting schools but not from exchanging letters with pupils.

Now our son and daughter have their own homes (in south London and north Norway) my wife and I divide the house – she to paint, I to write. I sit where the sun comes in through the window.

We had a splendid Westie called Snoopy who could read thoughts, but old age got him in the end. No pets now.

Date and place of birth:
31st March 1928
Barnton, Cheshire
Contact address:
18 McKenzie Road
Broxbourne
Hertfordshire EN10 7JH

Selected titles

Tom's Private War – World War 2 adventures (Puffin)

Never Kiss Frogs (Puffin)

The Third Class Genie (HarperCollins)

Smart Girls – folk tales of adventurous girls retold (Walker Books)

Swapper (Egmont/Mammoth)

Extract

Far above their heads, at the top of a kind of chimney, was daylight.

"Another way out," shouted Tom, excited.

"Yeah, and you know what," said Scouser. "We go out that way and they'll think we're still under here. What d'you reckon?"

"Smashing!" Then Tom stopped. "How do we get up, though? It's too high."

"We do like the steeplejacks. Put your back on one side and your feet on the other and walk up. Watch."

As Tom stared, he saw, by the faint light above, Scouser's body bent double, working his way up the chimney. Soon his climbing form blocked out the day.

"Come on!" his muffled voice commanded.

Tom followed, heaving and straining with back and feet spitting out the dirt that Scouser's boot showered on him.

From *Tom's Private War* (Puffin)

Favourite book: The latest Terry Pratchett
Favourite colour: Deep red or blue
Favourite food: Anything that my wife cooks: grilled trout, or risotto, or paprika chicken or …
Favourite word: I like them all
Favourite memory: Fishing in an Arctic lake in gentle grey light at 3 am.
Where do your ideas come from? Memories of my own young days. Stories my son and daughter told me of the time they were at school in inner London.

Things told me by tens of thousands of pupils I've met over nearly 30 years. In the army and afterwards, I lived and worked in 14 different countries – the Middle East taught me most. Ideas come easily, they take you by surprise. The difficult bit is what to do with them when they arrive.
What else might you have been? A farm worker, or a railwayman. But in fact it had to be something to do with words.

Robert Leeson

Joan Lingard

I WAS BORN IN EDINBURGH but went to live in Belfast when I was 2 years old and stayed there until I was 18. I attended a state primary school and at the age of 11 I won a scholarship to a girls' school, Bloomfield Collegiate. It was a small school then and it was somewhat eccentric, run by two sisters who insisted that we wore headgear at all times and did not speak to boys in the street. The staff were rather eccentric also, which in retrospect I see gave me material to write about. When a Geman woman joined the staff towards the end of World War 2 we immediately thought she must be a spy. Three of us followed her round Belfast with notebooks, recording her movements, and making her life miserable, no doubt. There was something about her that we did not know. Learning it later, and to make amends perhaps, I wrote *The File on Fraulein Berg*.

I was crazy about books as a child. I haunted the local library, a poor affair where the books were ancient, tattered and sometimes torn, and stained with the remnants of previous readers' meals. Through the splodges I read Enid Blyton, the 'Chalet School' books, Biggles and 'Just William'. Then one day, having nothing to read, nothing to do and thus feeling bored, I kept pestering my mother, who finally suggested I write a book of my own, and that was what I did.

Date and place of birth:
Edinburgh, Scotland
Contact address:
David Higham Associates
5–8 Lower John Street
Golden Square
London W1R 4HA
www.joanlingard.co.uk

Selected titles

Kevin and Sadie quintet (Puffin)

The File on Fraulein Berg (Hodder Children's Books)

Tug of War (Puffin)

Natasha's Will (Puffin)

Me and My Shadow (Puffin)

Extract

In former times the house had been full of people and noise. The doorbell had rung constantly. Her [Natasha's] mother and grandmother had entertained in the salon, serving tea, in small decorated teapots, made with hot water from the pot-bellied copper samovar that steamed gently in a corner for most of the day. With it, they had offered cakes, gooey meringues, crisp little honey and almond cakes, chocolate profiteroles, coffee and walnut cake.

Now there were no cakes in the house. The shop on the Nevsky Boulevard was closed. The doorbell didn't ring. It was quiet and still in the hall and corridors. People spoke in lowered voices in case any enemy might be listening. For it seemed that there were thousands out there baying for their blood. The sound of their cries was terrifying.

From *Natasha's Will* (Puffin)

Favourite book: *Pride and Prejudice* by Jane Austen
Favourite colour: Blue
Favourite food: Fish
Favourite word: Synchronicity
Favourite place: My home
Where do your ideas come from? My ideas come in so many different ways – it's difficult to list them all. Some, like *The File on Fraulein Berg* and *Kevin and Sadie* came from my Belfast childhood. Others, such as *Tug of War* and *Between Two Worlds,* came from my husband's childhood as a refugee fleeing from Latvia at the end of World War 2. Some are inspired by places – *A Secret Place* by Spain, *Natasha's Will* by St Petersburg. And then, at times, an idea will come just out of the blue, so it seems, as did *Me and My Shadow*.

Joan Lingard

Penelope Lively

I WAS BORN AND GREW UP IN EGYPT and did not go to school until I came to England, aged 12. Before that, I had lessons at home and mainly just read and read and read – Greek and Norse mythology, the Bible, *The Arabian Nights*, Dickens, anything that came to hand. When I was 12 I had to go to boarding school, where I was miserable for four years. One of the punishments in this terrible school was to be sent to the library to read a book for an hour – that was what the teachers thought of reading! Now I have four grandchildren, who are all perfectly happy at schools where books come first and foremost.

I work in a light sunny room full of books and papers and pictures, with a window overlooking the street so that I can look out at people passing when I get stuck with my writing.

Date and place of birth:
17th March 1933
Cairo, Egypt
Contact address:
David Higham Associates
5–8 Lower John Street
Golden Square
London W1R 4HA
www.penelopelively.net
www.penelopelively.com
www.penelopelively.co.uk

Selected titles

The Ghost of Thomas Kempe

A Stitch in Time

Uninvited Ghosts

The House in Norham Gardens

The Whispering Knights

All published by Egmont

Extract

James Harrison and his mother turned out of Ledsham's main street into a lane that ran between terraced cottages. The lane ended abruptly at a gate and became a footpath, which disappeared in a landscape of fields and trees, ridged with the dark lines of hedges. Their own cottage stood at the end; the last house in Ledsham. It was called East End Cottage and they had been living there for two weeks.

James walked five paces behind his mother, carrying her shopping basket, which he disliked because it banged against his bare legs and scratched him where the cane was broken. Also it had things like ladies' tights and cabbages sticking out of it, which was embarrassing. Tim, the dog, walked ten paces behind James. James looked back at him and tried to imagine him as one of those large, shaggy, responsible-looking dogs that carry folded-up newspapers and shopping baskets. Tim, squat, square and mongrel, grinned back, independent and unobliging.

From *The Ghost of Thomas Kempe* (Egmont)

Favourite book: *Alice in Wonderland* and *Alice Through the Looking Glass* by Lewis Carroll
Favourite colour: Green
Favourite food: Avocado pears
Favourite place: West Somerset, which has red earth and deep narrow lanes and tipping hills and buzzards and wonderful starry skies at night.

Where do your ideas come from? My ideas come from what I see and hear and read.
What else might you have been? A really good gardener.

Penelope Lively

Wes Magee

I WAS A SCHOOLBOY IN SHEFFIELD and Ilford, Essex where I read lots of books by Captain W.E. Johns (Biggles), Enid Blyton and Richmal Crompton (the William stories). Writing for me commenced in a barrack room in Germany when I was doing National Service, and I've been creating poems and plays ever since. For years I worked as a primary school teacher in Wiltshire, Hertfordshire and Yorkshire, but am now a full-time author living on top of the North York Moors (snowy in winter!). I work in an old caravan at the bottom of my large, wild garden through which Thorgill-beck tumbles down a series of waterfalls. Pets? Bracken, a collie dog, and Rusty, a rescued cat and dozens of fish in a huge pond.

Date and place of birth:
20th July 1939
Greenock, Scotland
Contact address:
Crag View
Thorgill
Rosedale Abbey
North Yorkshire
YO18 8SG
01751 417633

Selected titles

The Boneyard Rap, and other poems (Hodder Children's Books)

The Phantom's Fang-tastic Show – poems (OUP)

The Legend of the Ragged Boy – picture book (Andersen Press)

The Spookspotters of Scumbagg School – story (Orchard Books)

The Very Best of Wes Magee – poems (Macmillan Children's Books)

Extract

"Who," asked my mother,
"helped themselves to the new loaf?"
    My two friends and I
    looked at her,
    and shrugged.

"Who," questioned my mother,
"broke off the crust?"
    Three pairs of eyes
    stared at the loaf
    lying on the kitchen table.

"Who," demanded my mother,
"ate the bread?"
    No one replied.
    You could hear
    the kitchen clock. Tick. Tock.

And even now I can taste it,
crisp, fresh, warm from the bakery,
    and I'd eat it again
    if I could find a loaf
    like that, like that ...

From Morning Break, and Other Poems (CUP)

Favourite book: *The Castle of Adventure* by Enid Blyton
Favourite colour: Blue
Favourite food: Spaghetti Bolognese
Favourite word: Winner!
Favourite memory: Climbing Slieve Donard (the highest mountain in Northern Ireland) and standing on the summit with the Mourne Mountains all around and the Irish Sea far below.
Where do your ideas come from? My ideas come from anywhere and everywhere, but often from incidents or events that happened many years ago ... as in the poem 'Who?'.
What else might you have been? A winger with Sheffield Wednesday ... or a spin bowler ... or a dealer in antiques and rare books.

Margaret Mahy

I AM A NEW ZEALANDER. I have made my living as a writer for about 32 years. writing books, television scripts, articles and poems. I began writing when I was 7 years old.

I read all sorts of things, but I particularly loved adventurous stories – books like *Treasure Island* and *King Solomon's Mines*.

I was the oldest of five children. We had 26 cousins in the town we lived in, so we were a big straggling family. I have one grandson in London and five grandchildren (including twins) who live just down the road from me. I have a dog and two cats. My grandchildren, the cats and the dog come into my stories in all sorts of ways – often disguised. Sometimes I don't even know they are there until I read the stories after I have printed them out.

A writing life is hard work – but it is full of surprises. I do get tired at times, but I am never bored, and that is always a good thing.

Date and place of birth:
21st March 1936
Whakatane, New Zealand
Contact address:
23 Merlincote Crescent
Governors Bay
New Zealand
margaret.mahy@xtra.co.nz

Selected titles

The Great White Man-eating Shark – picture book (Puffin)

The Man whose Mother was a Pirate – picture book (Puffin)

A Villain's Night Out – middle school (Penguin)

The Changeover – young adult (Puffin)

Memory – young adult (Collins Flamingo)

Extract

My father was a bridge builder. That was his business – crossing chasms, joining one side of the river with the other.

When I was small, bridges brought us bread and books, Christmas crackers and coloured pencils – one-span bridges over creeks, two-span bridges over streams, three-span bridges over wide rivers. Bridges sprang from my father's dreams threading roads together – girder bridges, arched bridges, suspension bridges, bridges of wood, bridges of iron or concrete. Like a sort of hero my father would drive piles and piers through sand and mud to the rocky bones of the world. His bridges became visible parts of the world's hidden skeleton. When we went out on picnics it was along roads held together by my father's works. As we crossed rivers and ravines we heard each bridge singing in its own private language. We could hear the melody but my father was the only one who understood the words.

From a short story, 'The Bridge Builder', *The Door in the Air and Other Stories* (J.M. Dent)

Favourite book: *Where the Wild Things Are* by Maurice Sendak
Favourite colour: Green
Favourite food: Salad sandwiches
Favourite word: Mysterious (I use it all the time)
Favourite memory: Seeing my daughters when they were first born.
Where do your ideas come from? Nowadays nearly every story I write begins with something that has really happened around me, something I have smelt or heard or seen.
What else might you have been? I worked for many years as a children's librarian during the day. I always felt really triumphant when I felt I had found the right book for the right person.

Margaret Mahy

Jan Mark

I CAN HARDLY REMEMBER A TIME when I couldn't read and as soon as I could read I started to write – long before I went to school. I *wanted* to read and write; nobody had to nail me to the table. It was different with maths. When I was 7 I got the use of my father's typewriter, and I still work on a typewriter. People keep telling me a computer would save me a lot of time, but writing isn't about saving time and a computer would not make me a better writer.

When I was 12 I hijacked all the family's library tickets and every Saturday I borrowed 12 books to see me through the following week. When I wasn't reading I was writing – in my spare time I squeezed in some school work. I wouldn't recommend that these days, but as it turned out I was training myself for the way I needed to go.

Now I write full-time; I've just clocked up my quarter century. I have an office in the house where I type but I write my first drafts long-hand on the kitchen table where the light is good. This is why everything is covered in cat footprints. My cats park themselves exactly where I am writing.

Date and place of birth:
22nd June 1943
Old Welwyn
Hertfordshire
Contact address:
98 Howard Street
Oxford OX4 3BG

Selected titles

Strat and Chatto – picture book (Walker Books)

Lady Longlegs (Walker Books)

They Do Things Differently There (Red Fox)

The Eclipse of the Century – older/adult (Scholastic)

The Lady with Iron Bones (Walker Books)

Extract

Robin was four years old and he looked a lot younger, probably because nothing ever happened to him. Auntie Lynn kept no pets that might give Robin germs, and never bought him toys that had sharp corners to dent him or wheels that could be swallowed. He wore balaclava helmets and bobble hats in the winter to protect his tender ears, and a knitted vest under his shirt in summer in case he overheated himself and caught a chill from his own sweat. "Perspiration," said Auntie Lynn.

His face was as pale and flat as a saucer of milk, and his eyes floated in it like drops of cod-liver oil. This was not so surprising as he was full to the back teeth with cod-liver oil; also with extract of malt, concentrated orange-juice and calves-foot jelly. When you picked him up you expected him to squelch, like a hot-water bottle full of half-set custard.

From *Nothing to be Afraid of* (Puffin)

Favourite book: *Hamlet* by William Shakespeare
Favourite colour: Yellow
Favourite food: Seafood
Favourite word: Nogoodnik
Favourite place: Heathrow Airport
Where do your ideas come from? The first thing you learn if you write for a living, as I do, is that you can get a story out of anything. So, my ideas come from anywhere, real life mainly, books, television, movies … I don't mean that I steal the plots, I just see something that starts me thinking.

What else might you have been? I wanted a musical training but I went to art school instead and ended up as a teacher. I might still be one if I hadn't started writing. I love teaching and I still spend a lot of time in schools working in class and with teachers. When I was a student I worked in a pub. I really enjoyed that – and later on I wrote a book about it.

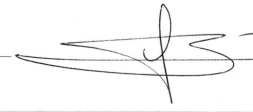

Geraldine McCaughrean

I HAVE A VERY CLEVER BROTHER called Neil. When I was young, everything he did, I wanted to do. So when, at 14, he had a book published, that became my great ambition. I was also very shy and timid. (I still am.) The one place I dared to have adventures was in my imagination, writing stories.

Dad was a fireman, Mum was a teacher. We did not have television until I was 9. You can imagine how exciting it was when we got one.

As I grew up, I went on writing – never really expecting to get published. I did a lot of jobs – secretary, teacher, journalist, sub-editor. I wrote as I travelled to and from work. Now I stay home all day and write. It's great, but it seems odd to earn a living by having so much fun. Sometimes I go into nearby schools to talk about being a writer, play story-making games and find out what the really important people – the readers – are thinking.

I have written over a hundred books, mostly for children, some for adults; also a play for radio and 50 little plays for schools. Maybe you'd like to act one. They are for about Year 5 upwards. Nowadays, I have an 12-year-old daughter to read my stories; a husband to check them; and a puppy, Daisy, to eat them.

Date and place of birth:
6th June 1951
Enfield, North London
Contact address:
David Higham Associates
5–8 Lower John Street
Golden Square, London
W1R 4HA

Selected titles

Stop the Train – 10+ (OUP)

Britannia: 100 Stories from British History – 8+ (Orion Children's Books)

100 World Myths and Legends – 8+ (Dolphin)

Gilgamesh – 8+ (OUP)

A Pack of Lies – 9+ (OUP)

Extract

Gilgamesh covered his friend over with a sheet of silk, carefully, precisely, meticulously. Then he smashed everything precious, everything beautiful, ripping down hangings, hurling ornaments out of the window. He tore out his hair and pulled his clothes in shreds, twisting his knuckles white in their rich fabrics.

Then, when the rage was past, he sat down again by his friend, panting, one hand on the silk. "Wake up now. Please wake up."

The whole household gathered outside the door, anxious, whispering, calling out …

From *Gilgamesh* (OUP)

Favourite book: *Tales of the Early World* by Ted Hughes
Favourite colour: Blue
Favourite food: Duck à l'orange
Favourite word: Suddenly
Favourite memory: The birth of my daughter Ailsa
Where do your ideas come from? Only twice have I based books on personal experience (*Too Big* and *Noah and Nelly*); but there is usually some grain of fact at the heart of my novels – something I have read about or seen on TV. Then I let imagination take over. I never base characters on real people.
What else might you have been? I suppose I would have gone on muddling through the publishing business (still writing for my own pleasure). But I would have liked also to be a photographer, capturing moments of time and images in much the same way as I try to do when I write.

Roger McGough

BEING GOOD AT DRAWING AT SCHOOL, I wanted to be an artist. But instead of going to art college I went to university (in Hull), where I began writing poems (I've no idea why!).

I was a teacher for 3¹/₂ years before taking early retirement and becoming a professional writer/singer/actor with a group called The Scaffold. When the group broke up after ten years I was able to earn my living as a poet.

I have three sons and a daughter and live near the river in London.

Date and place of birth:
9th November 1937
Liverpool
Contact address:
Penguin UK
80 Strand
London WC2R 0RL
www.rogermcgough.org.uk

Selected titles

Bad Bad Cats – poetry (Puffin)

The Ring of Words – edited anthology (Faber)

An Imaginary Menagerie – poetry (Puffin)

Lucky – poetry (Puffin)

Good Enough to Eat – poetry (Puffin)

Extract

The Missing Sock

I found my sock
beneath the bed.
"Where have you been
all week?" I said.

"Hiding away."
the sock replied.
"Another day on your foot
and I would have died!"

From *Pillow Talk* (Puffin)

Favourite book: A dictionary
Favourite colour: Green
Favourite food: Pasta
Favourite word: Liverpool
Favourite place: Deya in Mallorca where we holiday as a family.
Where do your ideas come from? From reading and listening. But the more you write the more ideas come to you. It is the very act of writing that stimulates my imagination.
What else might you have been? If I had not been a writer I would like to have been an illustrator. But if I had been an illustrator I would have wanted to be a writer.

Adrian Mitchell

MY MOTHER AND FATHER READ to me and my older brother Jimmy every night and I loved the books they read – all the Beatrix Potter stories, *The Wind in the Willows* and *Treasure Island*. Later I read everything I could find, especially the 'Just William' books.

My first play was produced at school when I was 9 years old – it was called *The Animals' Brains Trust*. And my latest book is a collection of poems about animals written from the point of view of my Golden Retriever, Daisy. Daisy and I call our book *Zoo of Dreams*.

I have five grown-up children and seven grand-children. I love good theatre, jazz and paintings and I hate bullying and war.

Date and place of birth:
24th October 1932
near Hampstead Heath
London
Contact address:
14 Brookfield Park
London
NW5 1ER
www.adrianmitchell.co.uk

Selected titles

Balloon Lagoon – poems (Orchard Books)

Zoo of Dreams – animal poems (Orchard Books)

Nobody Rides the Unicorn – story (Doubleday)

A Poem a Day – anthology (Orchard Books)

My Cat Mrs Christmas (Orion Children's Books)

Favourite book: *Songs of Innocence and Experience* by William Blake
Favourite colour: Sky blue
Favourite food: Indian curry, Full English breakfast, Martian ice-cream
Favourite word: Animals
Favourite place: Hampstead Heath with my parents, my wife, my children, my grand-children and my dogs.

Where do your ideas come from? From dreams, from friends, from listening to conversations on buses and trains, from TV, from daydreams, from watching animals and reading newspapers. Or sometimes I'm asked to write a play based on *The Lion, The Witch and the Wardrobe* or the *Alice* books – and I often say Yes.

What else might you have been? I would have been a rock 'n' roll singer or a blues shouter – but I couldn't pass the exams.

Extract

The Woman of Water

There once was a Woman of Water
Who refused a Wizard her hand;
So he took the tears of a statue
And the weight from a grain of sand,
And he squeezed the sap from the comet
And the height from a cypress tree,
And he drained the dark from midnight
And he charmed the brains from a bee;
And he soured the mixture with thunder
And he mixed it with ice from Hell;
And the Woman of Water drank it down –
And she changed into a well.

There once was a Woman of Water
Who was changed into a well;
And the well looked up at the Wizard –
And down, down, down that Wizard fell.

From *Balloon Lagoon* (Orchard Books)

Adrian Mitchell

peace

Tony Mitton

I'VE ALWAYS LOVED STORIES, poems, songs and pictures. When I was about 9 we had to learn poems by heart at school. I found I could do it quite easily and liked the patterns of rhythm and rhyme they were made with. I also enjoyed writing poems and stories when we were asked to, and started to do it on my own as a hobby. Even then I wanted to be a writer, but didn't know how to become one "properly".

Later in life, as a primary teacher, I did lots of reading and writing with my pupils and grew very familiar with the world of children's books. When my own children came along I read with them a lot and started to write poems and rhymes for them. At about 40 I started to try and get my work published. Then the work really began …

Date and place of birth:
10th January 1951
Tripoli, North Africa
Contact address:
41 Sturton Street
Cambridge CB1 2QG
tonymitton@btinternet.com

Selected titles

Plum – poems (Scholastic Children's Books)

The Red and White Spotted Handkerchief – poems and narrative verse (Scholastic Children's Books)

Big Bad Raps – 'Rap Rhymes' series (Orchard Books)

Where's my Egg? – 'Flip Flap' book (Walker Books)

Flashing Fire Engines – 'Amazing Machines' series (Kingfisher)

Extract

Plum

Don't be so glum,
plum.
Don't feel beaten.
You were made
to be eaten.
But don't you know
that deep within,
beneath your juicy flesh
and flimsy skin,
you bear a mystery,
you hold a key,
you have the making of
a whole new tree.

From *Plum* (Scholastic Children's Books)

Favourite book: *Collected Poems for Children* by Charles Causley, illustrated by John Lawrence
Favourite colour: Green
Favourite food: Bread
Favourite word: Oh!
Favourite place: Here and now
Where do your ideas come from? My ideas come from anywhere and everywhere. Out in the world. Inside my head. From books, places, things, words, conversations, dreams, telly, sights and sounds. All kinds of mood and experience. I try to be open to all the stuff life throws up, then kind of control bits of it with poems – spells.
What else might you have been? A musician, singer, actor, illustrator, dancer, conjuror or story-teller. Or possibly a hermit or monk.

Tony Mitton

Bel Mooney

I WENT TO SCHOOL IN LIVERPOOL until I was 14, then to Trowbridge High School, Wiltshire. After that I did my English degree at University College London. I became a successful journalist right away and worked for many national magazines and newspapers. But when I had our children (Daniel was born in 1974 and Kitty in 1980) I began to shift towards writing books for adults and children. Books had always been at the centre of my life since I was small, so this seemed the right step.

Now I live on a hill farm outside Bath and write surrounded by fields that have no nasty chemicals put on them. We have two dogs, four cats, three horses, chickens, cows and sheep. Apart from writing my books I still do some journalism and also make programmes for BBC Radio 4. My hobbies are reading, seeing friends and riding on the back of a Harley Davidson motorcycle.

Date and place of birth:
8th October 1946
Liverpool
Contact address:
David Higham Associates
6–8 Lower John Street
Golden Square
London W1R 4HA
www.bel-mooney.co.uk

Selected titles

The Voices of Silence (Collins Educational)

It's Not Fair! (Mammoth)

But You Promised! (Mammoth)

Why Me? (Mammoth)

It's Not My Fault! (Mammoth)

Extract

It was a normal, quiet Sunday, the day after my birthday. I was doing my homework, Mama was mending her tights, my father was on his hands and knees replacing the wick of the paraffin stove. As a result, we were rather cold. I even had my black muffler on. The silky red scarf was laid carefully in the top drawer in my bedroom, for special occasions. Mama had made a potato and onion soup for lunch, and already the savoury smell filled the room, making me hungry.
Suddenly there was a knock. My father looked up sharply, my mother stared anxiously at him, and I glanced at the clock on the wall, wondering who would come at this time on a Sunday morning. Then I felt a huge leap of excitement. It would be Alys – I was sure of that. Alys knew it was my birthday; she must be feeling sorry that we had quarrelled and had decided to come over to make friends.
I jumped up. "I expect it's Alys," I said, and then my parents relaxed once more, like puppets when the puppet master slackens the strings.

From *The Voices of Silence* (Collins Educational)

Favourite book: *Middlemarch* by George Eliot
Favourite colour: Blue/purple
Favourite food: Goat's cheese and salad
Favourite word: Wonderful
Favourite memory: Watching my parents ballroom dancing in the Tower Ballroom, Blackpool
Where do your ideas come from? My ideas come from my family and things overheard. Faces in the street. Odd newspaper stories. Memories buried but bursting to be revived. Ideas about good and bad, joy and pain, hope and despair … and love, God and death. Good times and fun and laughter!
What else might you have been? I think I'd have probably gone into teaching, which is one of the finest professions in the world. I'd have taught English literature, because great books can change people's lives.

Bel Mooney

Michael Morpurgo

I WENT AWAY TO SCHOOL when I was very young. I loved rugby and singing, and hated school work. I didn't start writing until I was nearly 30, after several years' teaching. I discovered I could "tell" stories quite well aloud to my class, so I decided to try writing them down.

I am now very old (57 years), very married (37 years), father of 3 and grandfather of 6. I live and work on a farm down in deepest Devon, where my wife Clare and I have set up farms for city children. They have been going for 25 years now. There are three where over 3,000 city children a year come to live and work for a week of their school term. Lots of muck and magic!

Date and place of birth:
5th October 1943
St Albans, Hertfordshire
Contact address:
Langlands
Iddesleigh, Winkleigh
Devon EX19 8SH
mab.purgo@virgin.net

Selected titles

The Butterfly Lion (Collins)

Kensuke's Kingdom (Mammoth)

The Wreck of the Zanzibar (Mammoth)

Why the Whales Came (Mammoth)

Out of the Ashes (Macmillan Children's Books)

Extract

Butterflies only live short lives. They flower and flutter for just a few glorious weeks, and then they die. To see them, you have to be in the right place at the right time. And that's how it was when I saw the butterfly lion – I happened to be in the right place, at just the right time. I didn't dream him. I didn't dream any of it. I saw him, blue and shimmering in the sun, one afternoon in June when I was young. A long time ago. But I don't forget. I mustn't forget. I promised them I wouldn't.

From *The Butterfly Lion* (Collins)

Favourite book: *The Old Man and the Sea* by Ernest Hemingway
Favourite colour: Red
Favourite food: Prawns
Favourite word: Peewit
Favourite place: Home
Where do your ideas come from? I look. I listen. I read. I learn. I have my ideas detectors – eyes, ears, all my senses in receiver mode all the time. I just glean from life. Then I weave my stories out of those realities to make a different kind of reality.

What else might you have been? Who knows? An actor probably. My mum was and my dad is still. I love the sound of words. I love drama. Yes, an actor. But then there's a lot of acting in writing, pretending you are someone inside your story, feeling as they might feel. So I am an actor after all – of sorts.

Brian Moses

I DIDN'T RELATE MUCH TO WRITING when I was at school. Most of the time I just wanted to kick a ball around and dream of playing for Spurs. But I did read a lot. Enid Blyton kick-started the habit. I wanted to be adventuring with the Famous Five. Then I moved on to the Jennings, Billy Bunter, William and Biggles series – after you'd enjoyed the first book there were tons more to look forward to.

Today I live in Sussex with my wife Anne and my two daughters Karen and Linette. I work in a room that I had built in my garden. It is full of books, computers and percussion instruments. Our pets are two nervous guinea-pigs and several fish. We once had a lop-eared rabbit who loved to play football!

These days I spend half my time writing at home and the other half travelling, visiting schools and performing my poems wherever there is an audience. I play percussion to emphasise the rhythms in lots of my poems and often feel I'm the modern equivalent of the medieval travelling jester! It's a great way to earn a living and I wouldn't change it.

Date and place of birth:
18th June 1950
Ramsgate, Kent
Contact address:
11 Barrow Rise
St Leonards-on-Sea
East Sussex TN37 7ST
redsea@freezone.co.uk
www.poetry.ndirect.co.uk

Selected titles

Barking Back at Dogs (Macmillan)

Don't Look at Me in that Tone of Voice (Macmillan)

Beetle in the Bathroom (Puffin)

I Wish I Could Dine with a Porcupine (Hodder Children's Books)

The Secret Lives of Teachers – editor (Macmillan)

Extract

December Moon

The moon has come out too soon,
it's still the middle of the afternoon
and the day shows no sign of darkness.

What is the moon doing,
sneaking into the sky when it's light?

What is the moon playing at?
Couldn't it sleep?
Has its alarm clock rung too soon?

Do we see the moon this early
in June or September?

Or does December bring a special moon,
a let's-get-these-nights-over-soon moon,
a can't-wait-for-Christmas-to-come moon?

From *Barking Back at Dogs* (Macmillan)

Favourite book: *Turtle Diary* by Russell Hoban
Favourite colour: Green
Favourite food: A recipe of my wife's – a fish dish with tomato, basil, garlic and rice
Favourite word: S-s-s-s-snake
Favourite place: New York – for its vibrancy and inspiration; and Scotland (the north-west Highlands) – for their tranquillity and grandeur.
Where do your ideas come from? Ideas come from anywhere and everywhere. An idea is a bit like a knock on the door; ignore the knocking and whoever it is goes away, ignore the idea and it disappears. I have written poems based on things I overhear people say, places I visit, newspaper reports, television, slogans, adverts, music, etc.
What else might you have been? I would probably still be teaching.

Beverley Naidoo

I WAS BROUGHT UP IN WHAT WAS KNOWN as one of the world's most openly racist countries. In my whites-only, girls-only convent, we were taught to answer only the teacher's questions. We were not meant to ask our own questions – and certainly not questions about racism. Our English teacher dictated pages of boring notes about Shakespeare and we had to learn them off by heart. It was only years later that I discovered how fantastic his plays were.

Our teachers were frightened of us thinking for ourselves. Some books stir you to think and we weren't encouraged to use a library. Our vice-principal even refused to sign my application to get a library card! She said that my school books should be enough for me. When I left school, I began to read whatever I could. I also hope the books I write now encourage lots of questions! My first book, *Journey to Jo'burg*, was actually banned in South Africa until the year after Nelson Mandela was released from jail. How crazy to think that you can ban ideas!

Date and place of birth: 21st May 1943 Johannesburg, South Africa
Contact address: Penguin UK, 80 Strand London WC2R 0RL www.beverleynaidoo.com

Selected titles

Journey to Jo'burg (Collins Modern Classics)

No Turning Back (Puffin)

The Other Side of Truth – Carnegie Medal 2000 (Puffin)

Out of Bounds – 7 short stories (Puffin)

Baba's Gift – picture book written with Maya Naidoo, illustrated by Karen Littlewood (Puffin)

Extract

Sade is slipping her English book into her schoolbag when Mama screams. Two sharp cracks splinter the air. She hears her father's fierce cry, rising, falling.

"No! No!"
The revving of a car and skidding of tyres smother his voice. Her bag topples from the bed, spilling books, pen and pencil on to the floor. She races to the verandah, pushing past Femi in the doorway. His body is wooden with fright.

"Mama mi?" she whispers.
Papa is kneeling in the driveway, Mama partly curled up against him. One bare leg stretches out in front of her. His strong hands grip her, trying to halt the growing scarlet monster. But it has already spread down her bright white nurse's uniform. It stains the earth around them.

A few seconds, that is all. Later, it will always seem much longer.

From *The Other Side of Truth* (Puffin)

Favourite book: *Roll of Thunder, Hear My Cry* by Mildred D. Taylor
Favourite colour: Rainbow colours
Favourite food: Paw-paw (papaya)
Favourite word: *ubuntu* (Xhosa) = *l'humanité* (French) = *humanity* (English)
Favourite memory: Playing as a child in a donga (a dry sandy riverbed) in Rustenburg, South Africa – and years later playing with our children beside a flowing stream in Yorkshire, England

Where do your ideas come from? From life – and being nosy about life. I am especially interested in how young people deal with big issues – like injustice.
What else might you have been? I was a teacher and an education adviser for many years. I told my mother I'd throw myself off a bridge rather than teach – so you never can tell!

Judith Nicholls

MY FIRST SCHOOL WAS A TINY, one-room church school on the east coast of Lincolnshire – I had to walk through a field of cows to reach it and for the first few days yelled at the gate to go home! I became rather a shy teenager and liked to write in secret: in that way I could work out in my own time what I *really* wanted to say. It wasn't until many years later, when my three children were beginning to grow up, that I began to write professionally. My first book (*Magic Mirror*) came out in 1985.

Home is an ancient cottage in a churchyard and I'm very lucky because two of our four grandchildren live just round the corner. We have no pets now (at one point there were nine when our children were small!) but baby wrens, thrushes, blackbirds, robins and frogs live around the garden. My study is decidedly chaotic: paintings and books all around the walls, paper, pencils, letters, notes, poems all over the desk – and often the floor too. I probably have dozens of idiosyncrasies but the first that comes to mind is that I always work on green paper! I love working on poems, gardening, walking, plotting secrets with my grandchildren. Dislikes? Injustice, dishonesty, loud music in shops, crème de menthe!

Date and place of birth:
12th December 1941
Westwoodside, Lincolnshire
Contact address:
Faber and Faber
3 Queen Square
London WCIN 3AU

Selected titles

Dragonsfire – poems 7–12 (Faber)

Storm's Eye – poems (OUP)

Someone I Like – poetry anthology (Barefoot Books)

Otherworlds – poetry anthology (Faber)

Midnight Forest/Magic Mirror – poems (Faber)

Extract

Polar Cub

This way, that way?
Step out,
little five-toe flat-foot,
squint-eye,
cave-dazed,
into the sun!

Eyes left,
ears right,
nose to the wind!

The coast is clear!
Run, roll, lollop;
winter's done!
Enjoy the pause;
make your mark
on this blank page –
the world is yours!

From *Storm's Eye* (OUP)

Favourite book: *The Christmas Miracle of Jonathan Toomey* by Susan Wojciechowski (at the moment)
Favourite colour: Bronze
Favourite food: Homemade wholemeal bread
Favourite word: Only one?!? Murmuring
Favourite place: My own "Secret Garden".
Where do your ideas come from? From people or things seen or heard, newspaper snippings, a memory, a film, a place … Often I have a request for a particular subject, an excellent challenge. Any

poem is *made*, so however the idea started, a long drafting process will follow.
What else might you have been? My first job was on a monthly women's magazine; later I taught for some years. As I've now been writing and running workshops for about 16 years probably I shall continue …!

Judith Nicholls

William Nicholson

I USED TO HATE SCHOOL BUSES because the seats were in pairs and I was afraid no one would want to sit beside me. All my school life I longed for friends but secretly felt I was alone. I don't believe I understood how to make friends until I was grown up. I was too needy. Children can be cruel to those who show too much need. So I read books and made friends with people in books; most of all, William. I spent all my pocket money at the second-hand bookshop in Seaford, buying William books. I still have them all.

My clumsy childhood now seems to me to have been a strange blessing. Today I have a beloved family of my own, and many close friends, and I earn my living as a writer. This is all I ever dreamed of, and I ask no more of life. And yet I'll never feel that I'm one of the golden ones, born to be loved and to succeed; and whenever I see a child alone and pretending not to mind, I shiver, and see myself again.

Date and place of birth:
12th January 1948
Tunbridge Wells, Kent
Contact address:
Egmont Books
239 Kensington High Street
London W8 6SA

Selected titles

The Wind Singer

Slaves of the Mastery

Firesong (to be published in May 2002)

The three volumes of 'The Wind on Fire'

All published by Egmont

Extract

This poem appears in *Firesong*, where it is written by one of the characters, Rufy Blesh. But of course it's really written by me.

No, I'm not sad
And though I say nothing
I want to talk.
I'm waiting for you to smile
Then I'll smile too
And we can begin.
Are you like me?
Does it go on for ever
Waiting to smile?

From *Firesong* (Egmont)

Favourites

I like different things at different times. There are some things that I've slowly come to realise I love very much, and I think always will:
Dawn – I'm an early riser, and try to watch every dawn, especially in autumn and spring.
Building sites – the process of construction.

Looking out of the window on long train journeys.
Home fires, and firelight in a room.
Long lazy dinners with good friends and good wine; and spring in England, most of all the month of May.

Jenny Nimmo

AS SOON AS I HAD LEARNED TO READ I seemed to eat books – I could never get enough of them. I was very fond of Beatrix Potter, Barbar the Elephant and Rudyard Kipling's *Just So Stories*. But apart from those, there weren't many children's books in our house, so I started reading grown-up books. Some of these were very peculiar and I tended to shock people with the strange vocabulary I was picking up. I don't think I really understood what I was saying.

My father died when I was 5 and my mother became very ill, so I spent many hours alone, or in strangers' houses. I started making up stories to entertain myself and then, at school, I began to write them down. But my teachers weren't very pleased with the things that I wrote. So I stopped. But I kept the stories in my head like sort of wicked secrets.

Now I can write and there's no one to stop me. I live in an old converted watermill in Wales. My husband is an artist and our three children are all grown up, although the youngest is still at university. I work in her bedroom which overlooks the river, and it's difficult not to watch the ducks and herons fishing, swimming and playing in the water.

Date and place of birth:
15th January 1944
Windsor, Berkshire
Contact address:
Henllan Mill
Llangynyw, Welshpool
Powys SY21 9EN
jennynimmo@aol.com

Selected titles

The Stone Mouse (Walker Books)

The Witch's Tears (HarperCollins)

The Snow Spider (Egmont)

The Dragon's Child (Hodder Children's Books)

The Rinaldi Ring (Egmont)

Extract

A flock of crows rose out of the wood and fluttered up through the darkening sky, sending a flurry of snow in their wake. Soft as feathers, the snowflakes whirled over the garden and began to settle on the children. They spread their arms, hoping to look like snowmen, but the wind turned sharper, and the snow rushed at them in icy clouds. And something sparkled in the snow; a circle of tiny stars whirled down from the sky. It fell at Dodie's feet. An icy necklace filled with rainbow colours. Dodie picked up the glistening string, "Look," she said, "crystals".

Theo touched them, gently. "Witch's tears," he murmured, "threaded on silver".

From *The Witch's Tears* (HarperCollins)

Favourite book: *Where the Wild Things Are* by Maurice Sendak
Favourite colour: Ultramarine
Favourite food: Toast and marmite
Favourite word: Hope
Favourite place: A beach in Kerry, southern Ireland: white sand, a turquoise sea and soft rainfall full of golden sunshine.
Where do your ideas come from? I'm a terrible eavesdropper and rather nosy, so I get a lot of ideas by listening to other people's conversations. I also like to scan newspapers for tiny bits of local news tucked away at the back. My best inspiration has probably been my children and their pets.
What else might you have been? I was once an actress but not a very successful one. I was also a floor manager in TV, but it was a rather physical job and I could not have done it forever. My favourite work was editing and directing programmes from other authors' books. But writing my own books is much more satisfying.

Jenny Nimmo

Jan Ormerod

I GREW UP IN A LITTLE TOWN in Western Australia with three big sisters. I loved drawing and standing on my head. As I got older I stood on my head less and drew more. Now I am very lucky because I can draw all day every day. I don't stand on my head any more.

I started writing and illustrating children's books when my daughters were little and I fell in love with the books they read, like Shirley Hughes's *Dogger*. Now my daughters are grown up, both at universities, so I live in Cambridge with my three cats (Dogger, Smog and the one without a name) for part of the year and spend lots of time in Australia, Portugal and America with my family and friends.

One of the great things about being an author and artist for children's books is that I can take my work and do it wherever I am.

Date and place of birth:
23rd September 1946
Western Australia
Contact address:
Laura Cecil Agency
27 Alwyne Villas
London
N1 2HG
macunlimited.net

Selected titles

Ms Macdonald has a Class (Bodley Head/Red Fox)

A Twist in the Tale – animal stories from around the world edited by Mary Hoffman (Frances Lincoln)

Miss Mouse's Day (Doubleday)

Goodbye Mouse – by Robie H. Harris (Simon and Schuster)

The Story of Chicken Licken (Walker Books)

Illustration

From *Ms Macdonald has a Class* (Bodley Head/Red Fox)

Favourite book: My diary. What a muddle my life would be without it.
Favourite colour: Grey.
Favourite food: Everything! Especially green grapes, yoghurt, lobster, nuts, mangoes, cheese and wine …
Favourite words: I love you, Mum.
Favourite memory: Working in the garden in the company of two kids, two cats, one rabbit, one guinea-pig and two little red hens, all following me about in the sunshine. Bliss.
Where do your ideas come from? From underneath cabbages, of course.

Gareth Owen

MY FATHER LOVED BOOKS and was keen that I should as well. He read to me often – *Treasure Island, Lorna Doone* and *The Master of Ballantrae.*

When I was between 9 and 11 my favourite books were *The Children of the New Forest, Masterman Ready, Black Beauty, Just William* and *Swallows and Amazons.*

I wasn't brilliant at school and left to join the Navy at 16. I did various jobs and ended up teaching at a secondary school in Ilford. That's when I started writing poems, for the children in my class. Later I wrote novels.

I try to tell the truth, which is not the easiest thing in the world to do. Writing novels is in some ways telling lies as well as the truth.

Date and place of birth:
15th March 1936
Ainsdale, Lancashire
Contact address:
Jan Powling
Speaking of Books
9 Guildford Grove
London SE10 8JY
Tel: 0208 692 4704

Selected titles

Collected Poems for Children (Macmillan Children's Books)

The Fox on the Roundabout (Macmillan Children's Books)

Rosie No-name and the Forest of Forgetting (OUP)

Omelette: A Chicken in Peril (Red Fox)

Extract

Unemployable

"I usth thu workth in the thircusth,"
He said
Between the intermittent showers that
emerged from his mouth.
"Oh," I said, "what did you do?"
"I usth thu catch bulleth in my theeth."

**From *Collected Poems for Children*
(Macmillan Children's Books)**

Favourite book: *There is a Happy Land* by Keith Waterhouse
Favourite colour: Blue
Favourite food: Italian
Favourite word: Bunny
Favourite place: A field in Batty's Farm surrounded by trees where we used to play football – we called it Hampden.
Where do your ideas come from? By picking up a pen and a sheet of paper and starting to write.

I have written a poem called 'Gold' which answers this question.
What else might you have been? Who knows! I'd have probably carried on lecturing in a teacher's training college for another 20 years and would have enjoyed it.

Gareth Owen

73

Brian Patten

I WAS THE LAST CHILD TO LEARN TO READ in my class at primary school. My interest in books began outside school. I grew up in a house that had a front parlour, a kitchen, a bedroom and a box room. It was one of many terraced houses, all gone now, and was shared by three, sometimes four, adults and myself. There were always comics and newspapers, but I remember only one book. I remember finding it and wondering what on earth it was doing on top of the cupboard (it was about a fox and called *Wild Alone*). Imagine my sense of wonder when I first visited a house a few doors away to discover a room overflowing with books. Frieda, our neighbour, was a very tall spinster who wore a moth-eaten fox-fur. She had hundreds of books, not arranged neatly on shelves but scattered all over the place.

I took to visiting her, mainly because I needed help with reading my comics. One day Frieda insisted on reading from a book of fairy tales. The story was 'The Little Mermaid'. It was the saddest and most beautiful story I'd ever heard, and from that moment I was hooked on books.

Date and place of birth:
7th April 1946
Liverpool
Contact address:
personal@brianpatten.co.uk
www.brianpatten.co.uk

Extract

Geography Lesson

Our teacher told us one day he would leave
And sail across a warm blue sea
To places he had only known from maps,
And all his life had longed to be.

The house he lived in was narrow and gray
But in his mind's eye he could see
Sweet-scented jasmine clinging to the walls,
And green leaves burning on an orange tree.

He spoke of the lands he longed to visit,
Where it was never drab or cold.
I couldn't understand why he never left,
And shook off our school's stranglehold.

Then half-way through his final term
He took ill and never returned.
He never got to that place on the map
Where the green leaves of the orange tree burned.

The maps were redrawn on the classroom wall;
His name forgotten, he faded away.
But a lesson he never knew he taught
Is with me to this day.

I travel to where the green leaves burn,
To where the ocean's glass-clear and blue,
To places my teacher taught me to love –
And which he never knew.

From *Juggling with Gerbils* (Puffin)

Selected titles

Gargling with Jelly (Puffin)

Juggling with Gerbils (Puffin)

Mr Moon's Last Case (Allen & Unwin)

The Story Giant (HarperCollins)

Armada (Flamingo)

Favourite book: *Tarka the Otter* by Henry Williamson
Favourite colour: Magenta
Favourite food: Suet pudding
Favourite word: Sea-fret
Favourite place: The ruins of an underwater city

Where do your ideas come from? The planet Zog.
What else might you have been? A travel writer.

Korky Paul

I WAS BORN INTO A FAMILY OF SEVEN CHILDREN. My real name is Hamish Vigne Christie Paul. I enjoyed a wild and privileged childhood in the African bushveldt.

I cannot remember ever having any hobbies, but do remember spending hours scribbling cartoons and reading comic books from a very early age. My mother took us regularly to the local library, where I remember reading the 'Hardy Boys' and 'Just William' books.

I scribbled my way through Durban Art School, and for four years worked hard at an advertising agency in Cape Town (where I also played battleships and raced office chairs).

In 1976 I fled to Europe and cruised the continent in a VW Kombi van emblazoned with the words Chocolat Lanvin. Months later I washed up in Greece and met a mad Scot, James Watt, who nervously commissioned me to illustrate a series of educational books teaching Greek children to speak the Queen's English. And so I began my itinerant career as a children's book illustrator.

Date and place of birth:
5th December 1951
Harare, Zimbabwe
Contact address:
The Old Coal Hole
43 Oakthorpe Road
Summertown
Oxford
OX2 7BD
01865 516556
illustrator@korkypaul.com
www.korkypaul.com

Selected titles

Winnie the Witch – by Valerie Thomas (OUP)

Captain Teachum's Buried Treasure – by Peter Carter (OUP)

Dragons, Dinosaurs, Monster Poems – by John Foster (OUP)

The Dog that Dug – by Jonathan Long (Random House)

Aesop's Funky Fables – by Vivian French (Puffin)

Illustration

From *Winnie Flies Again* by Valerie Thomas (OUP)

Favourite book: *Jock in the Bushveldt/ Strawpeter* (Shock-headed Peter)
Favourite colour: Blue
Favourite food: Biltong
Favourite word: Serendipity
Favourite place: New York
Where do your ideas come from? I suppose my ideas must come from observing life and from my head. I actually have no idea where.
What else might you have been? Playing jazz music in a Paris nightclub! Cooking seafood in my own café bar on the beach in Greece? A brain surgeon?

Gervase Phinn

I LOVED READING AND WRITING at school and every spare moment I seemed to have my nose in a book or I was jotting down ideas, snippets of conversations, little poems, anecdotes (and keeping a diary containing secret thoughts!). I was one of four children and had a very happy childhood. Mum would read with me every night, Dad would tell long, exciting stories and my older brothers and sister would play games with me. I am still mad about books. My children (Richard, Matthew, Dominic and Lizzie) call me a bibliomaniac!

As a child I loved reading Beatrix Potter, Biggles stories and Dan Dare comics. My very favourite book was *The Selfish Giant* by Oscar Wilde. These days I spend much of my time visiting schools, running courses for teachers and, of course, writing. I live in a large red-brick house with a greasy-grey slate roof and work in one of the bedrooms, which has been converted into a study. It has wall-to-wall bookcases crammed with books.

Date and place of birth:
27th December 1946
Rotherham
South Yorkshire
Contact address:
Penguin UK, 80 Strand
London WC2R 0RL

Selected titles

My Cat Cuddles – picture book for 5–8-year-olds (Child's Play International)

What's the Matter Royston Knapper? – short stories for 10–12-year-olds (Child's Play International)

It Takes One to Know One – poetry collection for 8–12-year-olds (Puffin)

The Franklin Watts Collection of Poems – *Don't Go Pet a Porcupine*, *The Dog Ate my Homework*, *I Gave my Love a Red, Red Nose* and *Are We Nearly There Yet?* – edited anthologies for 8–13-year-olds

The Other Side of the Dale – an autobiography for older readers/adults (Penguin)

Extract

Mr Lee Teaches Poetry

Our English teacher, Mr Lee,
Is very keen on poetry
And every morning he will say:
"We're going to write a poem today.
But please don't waste a lot of time,
In trying to make your poetry rhyme.
In writing there is nothing worse
Than striving desperately in verse
To fit words into the line,
Just to get a silly rhyme.
So remember in your poem today,
It doesn't have to rhyme
– you know!"

From *It Takes One to Know One* (Puffin)

Favourite book: Still *The Selfish Giant* by Oscar Wilde
Favourite colour: Red
Favourite food: Yorkshire pudding
Favourite word: Reverie
Where do your ideas come from? I get my ideas from books I have read and by keeping my eyes and ears open. I am not a television watcher.

Favourite place: My favourite place is Runswick Bay, North Yorkshire, with its muddle of old houses and cottages, curve of sandy beach and dark, looming cliffs.
What else might you have been? I was a teacher for 14 years, then a school inspector. I still teach and love working with young people so I would not choose to do anything else.

Gervase

Jan Pieńkowski

AT THE AGE OF 8, I wrote a story for my father's birthday about a man showing off, driving his horse and carriage – an early case of road rage? He comes a cropper. I drew the pictures as I wrote, and in the last one the man has a nasty bump on his head. A year later, I made a birthday card for my mother, the figures cut out of scraps of waste paper – all that was available in wartime.

At Cambridge, I spent my time designing shows and theatre posters, when I should have been studying Classics and English.

In my first publishing job – for Collins – I got the chance to art direct ads and book-jackets. I went on doing jackets for Jonathan Cape until one day the children's editor offered me my first book.

An early collaboration with Joan Aiken let me develop my childhood love of silhouettes.

When Meg and Mog flew over the horizon, I found myself working in partnership with Helen Nicoll, creating books where words and pictures are seamlessly merged.

I now draw exclusively in Photoshop on Applemac and find that my early lessons have proved an unexpectedly useful apprenticeship for working on screen.

Date and place of birth:
8th August 1936
Warsaw, Poland
Contact address:
Oakgates
45 Lonsdale Road
Barnes, London SW13 9JR
jan@oakgates-barnes.demon.co.uk

Illustration

Helen Nicoll and Jan Pieńkowski

From *Meg and Mog* (Puffin)

Selected titles

Haunted House (Walker Books)

Dinner Time (Piggy Toes Press)

Meg and Mog (Puffin)

Christmas (Heinemann)

Pizza (Walker Books)

Favourite book: *Bleak House* by Charles Dickens
Favourite colour: Blue
Favourite food: Pasta
Favourite word: Excelsior
Favourite place: Rome
Where do your ideas come from? Going for walks with the dogs; sitting by the river; chance remarks, and observing friends and neighbours.
What else might you have been? An architect or a scientist. These are the principal occupations of my family.

Chris Powling

I GREW UP IN A TINY HOUSE in south London not far from where I live today. My family wasn't at all posh or book-ish – but, to keep us quiet I think, my mum let us join the local library at an early age. This worked pretty well for my twin brother Pat and my little brother Terry. With me, though, the effect was magical. Straightaway, I fell in love with stories of every kind – true stories, half-true stories and stories that are better than true.

Amazingly, I found I could also earn my living from stories by talking and writing about them as a teacher and broadcaster. Later, I began to write them too …

My wife Jan, and my daughters Kate and Ellie, tell me that my own life story is more like a storylife. And they could be right! I hope every one of my readers is just as lucky in finding a job that's so much fun.

Date and place of birth:
16th February 1943
London
Contact address:
Speaking of Books
9 Guildford Grove
Greenwich
London SE10 8JY
jan@speakingofbooks.co.uk
www.chrispowling.co.uk

Selected titles

The Mustang Machine (Barn Owl Books)

The Phantom Carwash (Barn Owl Books)

My Sister's Name is Rover – picture-book series (A & C Black)

The Multi-million Pound Mascot (OUP)

The Book about Books (A & C Black)

Extract

Even a shark's name makes me shiver.
It seems to be saying:
SH – to hush us
AR – to swallow us
K – to snap shut on us!
Sharks haven't changed for millions of years.
They're like leftover dinosaurs …

From *Sharks* (OUP), but you'd better read the whole book to see how I change my mind about these amazing creatures.

Favourite book: *Treasure Island* by Robert Louis Stevenson
Favourite colours: Green and gold
Favourite food: Mashed potato
Favourite word: Holiday
Favourite place: Where I happen to be writing at the time – usually in Greenwich, south London, but often in a tiny hut halfway up a mountain in southern France.
Where do your ideas come from? My best ideas come when I'm in a dreamy yet wide-awake state of mind … but I make sure I've got a notebook handy to jot them down so I don't lose anything useful.
What else might you have been? Writing will always be my favourite job – but I also work as a freelance teacher, journalist and broadcaster (all of them to do with words, you'll notice) so any of these would keep me happy.

Chris Powling

Philip Pullman

PHOTO: JAMES PULLMAN

I WENT TO SCHOOL IN THE DAYS WHEN we learned Latin and poems by heart and the times table and the Kings and Queens of England. None of it did me any harm whatsoever.

I have a wife, two sons who are now grown up, two pugs who are not, a piano and far too many books; and I like drinking whisky and visiting art galleries and listening to music and making things. I wish I had more time.

Date and place of birth:
19th October 1946
Norwich
Contact address:
Scholastic
Commonwealth House
1–19 New Oxford Street
London WC1A 1NU

Extract

"Let's play kids and Gobblers!"
So said Lyra to Roger the Kitchen boy from Jordan College. He would have followed her to the ends of the earth.
"How d'you play that?"
"You hide and I find you and slice you open, right, like the Gobblers do."
"You don't know what they do. They might not do that at all."
"You're afraid of 'em," she said. "I can tell."
"I en't. I don't believe in 'em, anyway."
"I do," she said decisively. "But I en't afraid either. I'd just do what my uncle done last time he came to Jordan. I seen him. He was in the Retiring Room and there was this guest who weren't polite, and my uncle just give him a hard look and the man fell dead on the spot, with all foam and froth round his mouth."
"He never," said Roger doubtfully. "They never said anything about that in the Kitchen. Anyway, you en't allowed in the Retiring Room."

"Course not. They wouldn't tell servants about a thing like that. And I *have* been in the Retiring Room, so there. Anyway, my uncle's always doing that. He done it to some Tartars when they caught him once. They tied him up and they was going to cut his guts out, but when the first man come up with the knife my uncle just looked at him, and he fell dead, so another one come up and he done the same to him, and finally there was only one left. My uncle said he'd leave him alive if he untied him, so he did, and then my uncle killed him anyway just to teach him a lesson."

Roger was less sure about that than about Gobblers, but the story was too good to waste, so they took it in turns to be Lord Asriel and the expiring Tartars, using sherbet dip for the foam.

From *Northern Lights* (Scholastic)

Favourite book: *The Magic Pudding* by Norman Lindsay
Favourite colour: Green
Favourite food: Sausage and chips
Favourite word: Cascade
Favourite place: Walking in the hills
Where do your ideas come from?
All sorts of places:
I steal them . . .
Ideas Я Us . . .
Walking about with my eyes glazed and my mouth open . . .
The telly . . .
Other people's books . . .
What else might you have been?
An illustrator (I like to think!)

Selected titles

Northern Lights (Scholastic)

The Subtle Knife (Scholastic)

The Amber Spyglass (Scholastic)

Clockwork (Young Corgi)

I was a Rat! (Corgi)

Philip Pullman

Jane Ray

I HAVE ALWAYS MADE BOOKS AND DRAWN PICTURES – I used to do a series of 'Mr Teddy' books when I was 5 or 6; there were 30 or 40 of them complete with author/illustrator 'blurb' on the back cover. Art was my 'thing' at school – I loved it and it got me out of some things that I hated, like PE. I have always enjoyed working by myself – essential for any writer or illustator; we don't tend to be a gregarious bunch. I'm about to take delivery of a rather superior garden shed to work in. I used to work in the house until my children (Clara, Elly and Joe) demanded a room each. I'm really looking forward to getting down to work on the next book. A perfect day for me is just that – me and the paper, no interuptions, no meetings, no phone. Unless, of course, the ideas don't come in, in which case one invents interuptions – endless cups of coffee, long chatty phone calls, making the beds, doing the washing …

The books I enjoyed as a child were wide ranging – I loved Beatrix Potter, Brian Wildsmith, John Burningham; I read Milly Molly Mandy, *Tom's Midnight Garden*, *The Children of Greene Knowe*, and *Marianne Dreams* and of course *Alice* – the first book I remember being unable to put down.

Date and place of birth:
11th June 1960
Chingford, London
Contact address:
41 Greenham Road
London N10 1LN
020 8442 1748 (home)
0796 882 3044 (studio)
dtemple41@aol.com

Illustration

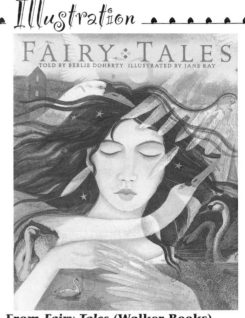

From *Fairy Tales* (Walker Books)

Selected titles

Fairy Tales – retold by Berlie Doherty (Walker Books)

The Happy Prince – by Oscar Wilde (Orchard Books)

Hansel & Gretel (Walker Books)

The Orchard Book of Love and Friendship – written by Geraldine McCaughrean (Orchard Books)

Can you Catch a Mermaid? – written and illustrated by Jane Ray (Orchard Books, September 2002)

Favourite book: *Fugitive Pieces* by Anne Michaels

Favourite colour: All colours – can't choose any one; it would be like choosing between my children!

Favourite food: Roast Sunday lunch with all the trimmings and the family there.

Favourite memory: Each of my children being introduced to their newborn brothers/sisters.

Where do your ideas come from? From folk tales, mythology, my children, dreams, things going on in the news, things I see around me – fragments that sometimes link up like beads on a string to form the 'necklace' of a story or picture.

What else might you have been? I was interested in teaching children with special needs and also in art therapy. If I hadn't pursued my career in children's books I'm pretty sure I would have been doing that. I enjoy visiting schools and working with children through my books.

Jane Ray

Shoo Rayner

MY FATHER WAS A BRITISH ARMY OFFICER, so we lived in exciting places around the world when I was young.

The best place was Aden, at the bottom of Arabia. It was very hot and we spent almost every day at the beach. My elder brother and sister and I would fly back to England to go to boarding school on "lollypop specials". These were planes filled with children who were also flying back to school. The flights were fun, but I wouldn't want to go to boarding school again.

I was a very lazy boy. I was good at day-dreaming! I am a bit dyslexic and couldn't write for toffee at school. In fact my handwriting is so bad that often even I can't read it!

It was only when I got a computer in the early 1980s that I found out that I could write, and I was able to read back what I had written!

I'd always written songs, so I suppose I had been writing all along. I still write songs; you can hear some of them on my website!

Date and place of birth:
15th December 1956
Kingston upon Thames
Surrey
Contact address:
shoo@shoo-rayner.com
www.shoo-rayner.co.uk
www.picturebooklibrary.com
www.picturebookradio.com
www.dark-claw.co.uk

Selected titles

The Ginger Ninja (Hodder Children's Books)

The Rex Files (Hodder Children's Books)

Super Dad (Hodder Children's Books)

Rock-a-doodle-do! (Orchard Books)

Treacle, Treacle, Little Tart (Orchard Books)

Illustration

From *The Ginger Ninja* (Hodder Children's Books)

Favourite books: *Where the Wild Things Are* by Maurice Sendak and *Northern Lights* by Philip Pullman
Favourite colour: Vermillion
Favourite food: Pasta
Favourite word: Sesquipedalian
Favourite place: West Kennet long barrow
Where do your ideas come from? Sometimes my ideas just appear as if by magic. Only later do I see where all the threads come from. Usually it is a word that sparks me off – that pulls all the threads together. It is a wonderful feeling when I get a good idea. I have to write it down quickly in case I forget. After that it's all down to hard work.
What else might you have been? I think I would have been a computer guru and would have become a dot com millionaire. I'm more interested in the artistic side of computers than in making a fortune.

John Rice

PHOTO: CLARE HAMILTON

THE PRIMARY SCHOOL I WENT TO, St Mary's in Saltcoats in Ayrshire, was demolished recently and new houses were built on the site. I enjoyed my years there as one of the teachers – a Mr Clinton – encouraged my interest in astronomy. We didn't have books in my house in Scotland but my favourite library book as a child was *1001 Questions Answered about Astronomy*. However, we did have lots of songs, stories, catches, riddles, and silly verses which we learned. These are known as "the oral tradition" and I call it up for my storytelling shows.

Later, at secondary school, another teacher – this time a languages teacher called Mr Melon – encouraged me to study French and Spanish. Later in life I took up other languages such as Russian and Arabic. Teachers can be very influential people!

I started writing stories when I was about 14 and I also wrote words and lyrics to tunes by a pop group called The Shadows (they were Cliff Richard's backing group at the time).

When I was about 23 or 24 I started publishing my poems in magazines and books. Since then I have published seven books for children and six for adults. I am well known as a performance poet and a storyteller as I do many performances in schools, libraries, arts centres, museums, sports centres and theatres.

Date and place of birth:
12th March 1948
Glasgow, Scotland
Contact address:
47 Hendley Drive
Cranbrook Kent TN17 3DY
johnandclarerice@yahoo.com
www.poetjohnrice.com

Selected titles

Bears Don't Like Bananas (Hodder Wayland)

An Odd Kettle of Fish (Macmillan Children's Books)

Down At The Dinosaur Fair (Kingscourt)

Scottish Poems (Macmillan Children's Books)

Extract

Rhyme-osaur the Dime-osaur

Out of a dark mine-osaur
at roughly half past nine-osaur
there came a sleepy steg-osaur
into the warm sunshine-osaur
he warmed his chilly spine-osaur
which made him feel divine-osaur
he nibbled on a pine-osaur
and drank a glass of wine-osaur
but then he saw a sign-osaur
which made him yelp and whine-osaur
it forecast his decline-osaur
his time had come to *die-nosaur*

From *Dreaming of Dinosaurs* (Macmillan Children's Books)

Favourite book: *The Third Policeman* by Flann O'Brien
Favourite colour: Blue (all shades, especially oceanic)
Favourite food: Cheese on toast (late at night)
Favourite word: Zoomballoomballistic
Favourite place: The Isle of Barra, a remote island in the Hebrides in Scotland.
Where do your ideas come from? My ideas come mainly from words having accidents. Sometimes you see words bumping into themselves or falling over one another. For example, I was driving along the road the other day and I saw an advert for a "photographer" then I saw the word "mahogany" outside the timber merchants. I liked putting them together to "mahogany photography"… it just sounds silly but great and I like the idea of a wooden person taking photos because you are supposed to stand still anyway!

Chris Riddell

I HAD A WONDERFUL ART MASTER at school who introduced me to the work of great illustrators like E.H. Shepard, William Heath Robinson, Arthur Rackham and Edmund Dulac.

I used to copy Tenniel's illustrations from the Alice books. I used to write and draw my own newspapers and produce my own comics, so I suppose it was natural that I should end up as a newspaper cartoonist and children's book illustrator (like Shepard and Tenniel).

When I'm not in the *Observer* offices, I work in my studio at the bottom of my garden, which is a converted coach house (with a hayloft and a stall for the horse!).

Date and place of birth:
13th April 1962
Cape Town, South Africa
Contact address:
sanctaphrax@hotmail.com

Selected titles

'The Edge Chronicles' – with Paul Stewart (Transworld)

'The Blobheads' – with Paul Stewart (Macmillan Children's Books)

Platypus (Penguin)

Something Else – written by Kathryn Cave (Penguin)

Juggling with Gerbils – poems by Brian Patten (Puffin)

Illustration

From *Beyond the Deepwoods*, Book 1 of 'The Edge Chronicles' (Corgi)

Favourite book: *Flat Stanley* by Jeff Brown
Favourite colour: Black
Favourite food: Avocado pears
Favourite word: Sanctaphrax
Favourite place: Table Mountain, Cape Town
Where do your ideas come from? My ideas come from my sketchbooks. I always have at least four sketchbooks on the go at any one time. Often I find ideas I jotted down years ago, come to life suddenly, e.g. *Platypus*.
What else might you have been? I would probably have been an accountant who doodled in the margins.

Chris Riddell

Philip Ridley

I WAS VERY SICK AS A CHILD. I suffered from – and still do! – asthma. Sometimes I was in an oxygen tent for days and days. This meant I did a lot of reading. My favourite things were comics. *Spider-Man*, *X-Men*, *Iron Man* – they were all my best friends. I also read a lot of horror novels and science fiction. My love of stories started there.

Also, I shared a bedroom with my younger brother, Tony. He was very nervous as a child. Lots of things would scare him, especially at night, so – as you can imagine – it took him ages to get to sleep. To help him calm down (to make him feel safe) I told him stories. I just made them up off the top of my head. The stories were about things from our neighbourhood (the East End of London, where I still live) with bits of comic fantasy and horror and science fiction thrown in. I guess this is where the roots of my style can be found.

Date and place of birth:
29th December 1964
London
Contact address:
Puffin Books
80 Strand
London WC2R 0RL

Selected titles

Mighty Fizz Chilla

Vinegar Street

Scribbleboy

Kasper in the Glitter

Krindlekrax

All published by Puffin

Extract

Wizard's Advice to Baby Dragon

Your breath is furnace.
Burn down doors.
Show your fangs
Sharpen claws.
Be fearless and wild
With daring desire.
Light up the dark!
Embrace your fire!

Published by permission of the author

Favourite book: *Stig of the Dump* by Clive King
Favourite colour: Black (with a hint of blue)
Favourite food: Chocolate biscuits (with a cup of tea)
Favourite word: Crocodile
Favourite place: My favourite place would be in a space capsule exploring the universe. I ain't been there yet, of course, but one day ... My favourite memory would be seeing my first Super Nova!

Where do your ideas come from? Karamazoo.
What else might you have been? An astronomer or an archaeologist or a total waste of space.

Tony Ross

I QUITE ENJOYED MY SCHOOL DAYS, not because of school. I was not good at or interested in schoolish things. I enjoyed the playtimes, lunch, going home, the holidays, the weekends, the friends and, of course, being that age. The end of the war seemed an exciting time, happy people rejoicing, and the promise of a new world.

I felt lucky to be youngish in the 50s and 60s too, great times.

Date and place of birth:
10th August 1938
London
Contact address:
Andersen Press
20 Vauxhall Bridge Road
London
SW1V 2SA

Illustration

From _Harold the Hairiest Man_ (Orchard Books)

Selected titles

I Want My Potty

I'm Coming to Get You

Foxy Fables

The Boy who Cried Wolf

Dr Xargle's Book of Earthlets

All above books and many more published by Andersen Press

Favourite books: The Rupert Bear books
Favourite colour: White
Favourite food: Lobster
Favourite word: Plop
Favourite memory: Warm summers long ago.
Where do your ideas come from? I don't know where my ideas come from, they just sneak up from behind. I think the things children say have a lot to do with it!

What else might you have been? A cowboy. I wanted to be one of those but my mother wouldn't let me go to America! I really wanted to be in Western films, so anything to do with acting or the stage would have been OK, although I could never remember the lines.

Nick Sharratt

PHOTO: © BOB CURTIS

WHEN I WAS A BOY I liked to draw in felt-tip pens. I must have got through hundreds of them, especially the black ones. I was 9 when I drew a big felt-tip picture of a market square and got to hold it up in assembly. That's when I decided that I was going to be a professional artist.

I loved it when the weekends came around and I could shut myself away in my bedroom with a bag of sweets and the radio and spend the whole two days drawing.

I drew very detailed pictures with lots going on and my favourite thing to work on was a really busy crowd scene, packed with people.

Now that I'm grown up, a few things have changed. I've swapped my felt-tip pens for sticks of charcoal, water-colour inks and a computer. I've got a proper studio to work in. And I get to draw each and every day! (But I still like to munch sweets and listen to the radio when I'm working.)

Date and place of birth:
9th August 1962
Bexleyheath
Contact address:
Scholastic
Commonwealth House
1–19 New Oxford Street
London WC1A 1NU

Selected titles

Ketchup on your Cornflakes? (Scholastic)

My Mum and Dad Make me Laugh (Walker Books)

Buzz Buzz Bumble Jelly (Scholastic)

The Time it Took Tom – written by Stephen Tucker (Scholastic)

Eat your Peas – written by Kes Gray (Random House)

Illustration

From *Buzz Buzz Bumble Jelly* (Scholastic)

Favourite book: *The Giant Jam Sandwich* by John Vernon Lord and Janet Burroway
Favourite colour: Bright yellow
Favourite food: Home-made trifle
Favourite word: Pumpkin
Favourite place: Swaledale in Yorkshire, if I want peace and quiet; and Brighton if I don't!
Where do your ideas come from? I can remember my childhood very clearly indeed, and a lot of the time I get my ideas from thinking about what interested me then.
What else might you have been? If I wasn't able to draw for a living I don't know what I'd do. I was a paperboy once, so perhaps I'd go back to doing that!

Nick Sharratt

Posy Simmonds

I LIVE AND WORK IN CENTRAL LONDON. I have drawn/written stories from the age of 4.

I grew up on a farm with cows, geese, ducks, chickens, dogs, cats, rats and mice. The house and attics were crammed with books and ancient magazines. I and my three brothers and sister read (almost) everything … including very sad Victorian children's books, Enid Blyton, Henty, Edward Lear, tons and tons of comics and an Enormous Veterinary Dictionary full of disgusting pictures of mange, boils etc.!

Date and place of birth:
1945
Berkshire
Contact address:
Peters Fraser & Dunlop
Drury House
34–43 Russell Street,
London
WC2B 5HA

Selected titles

Fred

Lulu and the Flying Babies

Freezing ABC

The Chocolate Wedding

Lavender

All published by Jonathan Cape/ Random House

Favourite book: *Sentimental Education* by Gustave Flaubert
Favourite colour: Blue, white, black – equally
Favourite food: Chocolate
Favourite word: Chocolate
Where do your ideas come from? My ideas come from brooding.
What else might you have been? I never wanted to be anything else – although learning how to make very complicated cakes might have been interesting.

Illustration

We growled at a tiger.....

Grrrh!

From *Lulu and the Flying Babies* (Jonathan Cape)

P.S.

Paul Stewart

WHEN I WAS 10, I won the school prize for diligence. It was a book: Norton Juster's *The Phantom Tollbooth*. From the moment I finished reading it the first time, I knew that I also wanted to be a writer. It was just so brilliant! It took a long time, but twenty-odd years later my first book, *The Thought Domain*, was published. Since then I have written more than fifty books, mostly for kids.

I live in a tall thin house near the coast with my wife and our two children, Joseph and Anna. Writing at home meant that I was lucky enough to spend a lot of time with them while they were growing up. We have a cat, Bindhi, and two goldfish, Goldie and Arsenal.

In 1992 I met up with the illustrator, Chris Riddell, because our sons were at the same nursery. Since then, as well as continuing to write books on my own, the pair of us have collaborated on various projects, including 'The Edge Chronicles'.

Date and place of birth:
4th June 1955
London
Contact address:
Contact me via the publisher of whichever book your school is using and enjoying.

Selected titles

Beyond the Deepwoods – Book 1 of 'The Edge Chronicles' (Corgi)

The Wakening (Yearling Books)

Adam's Ark (Puffin)

Silly Billy – No. 7 in 'The Blobheads' series (Macmillan Children's Books)

The Curse of the Gloamglozer – 'The Edge Chronicles' (Doubleday)

Extract

Twig's heart began to race. He looked round him wildly. There were eyes in the shadows. Yellow eyes. Green eyes. Red eyes. And all of them staring at him. "Oh no," he moaned. "What have I *done*?"

Twig knew what he had done. "Never stray from the path," Spelda had said. Yet that was *precisely* what he had done. Entranced by the silvery beauty of the Deepwoods, he had strayed from the safety of the path ...

From *Beyond the Deepwoods*, Book 1 of 'The Edge Chronicles' (Corgi)

Favourite book: *The Phantom Tollbooth* by Norton Juster
Favourite colour: Blue
Favourite food: Pesto
Favourite word: Yes
Favourite place: Holkham beach, Norfolk; a wide sandy bay surrounded by dunes and pine woods. As a boy I found the place magical.
Where do your ideas come from? The most difficult question of all! I have no idea – or rather I have lots of ideas. Some are stupid like "What if veruccas were conquering aliens", and never go any further. But some "What ifs" turn into stories.
What else might you have been? Probably a teacher. My mother was a teacher, my wife is a teacher. I used to teach English to foreign students. It was fun and enabled me to travel all over the world. I prefer writing, though!

Jeremy Strong

PHOTO: MARTIN SALTER

I LIKED PRIMARY SCHOOL and absolutely hated my grammar school. I began writing when I was about 16. I started with poems and then went on to stories. I eventually got my first book published when I was 27.

I have been married for 28 years and have two grown-up children. We have always liked cats and have had several over the years. Our present cat is black, fluffy and brain-dead. She is called Rubbish and she's very sweet.

I work in a small upstairs room that used to be a bedroom. It looks out over the garden and the fields to the North Downs. I'm very lazy and often find it hard not to sit there just staring out of the window all day! When I am writing I get noisy. I talk to myself out loud. I have arguments and I pull faces and wander around. It all helps me write the story! (It also keeps the cat entertained!)

Date and place of birth:
18th November 1949
New Eltham, London
Contact address:
Penguin Children's Books
80 Strand
London WC2R ORL
www.jeremystrong.co.uk

Selected titles

I'm Telling You, They're Aliens!
(Puffin)

The Hundred Mile an Hour Dog
(Puffin)

The Karate Princess Stories
(Puffin)

My Mum's Going to Explode!
(Puffin)

Problems with a Python
(Barrington Stoke)

Extract

Boy, you should have heard the row today! I thought the house would fall down round our ears. We've all been in Big Trouble with Mum.

The thing is, Mum's cooking has been all wonky for weeks now. She keeps giving us sausages to eat. She seems to have developed a craving for them. We're given sausages for breakfast, sausages for lunch and sausages for supper. It's driving us mad. Dad even pleaded with her, on his knees.

"Please, please, can we have something else to eat?"

"Sausages are very nice and I like them."

Granny says that when women are expecting a baby they sometimes go through a phase like this.

"When I was expecting Ronald, I spent a whole month eating nothing but soap and sardines."

"That's revolting, Granny!"

From *My Mum's Going to Explode!* (Puffin)

Favourite book: *The Jolly Postman* by Janet and Allan Ahlberg

Favourite colours: Blues and yellows

Favourite food: Artichokes with hollandaise sauce

Favourite word: Yes

Favourite place: Avery Hill Park, 25th April 1966

Where do your ideas come from? My ideas come from places, people, memories, dreams, words, walking, photographs – everywhere and anywhere, anytime.

What else might you have been? Very disappointed and fed-up (but I would also like to have been a Grand Prix driver or Tarzan).

Jonathan Stroud

THE FIRST STORY I REMEMBER WRITING was when I was 7. It was about some children who found a secret passage in a castle, outwitted two villains and got away with the treasure. It was so long that I ran out of paper. Soon after, I began drawing lots of comics that were full of spaceships, monsters and superheroes. When I was about 13, I started making up fantasy boardgames with a friend – every time one of us invented a game it would spur the other to dream up something better. This rivalry made us very productive.

At school I always read avidly – I was a big fan of Tolkien, C.S. Lewis, Diana Wynne Jones, R.L. Stevenson, Rudyard Kipling and Ruth Manning Sanders, who retold lots of folktales for children. When I write something now, I try to make it the kind of thing I would love to read myself – adventures full of danger and suspense.

Today I work in a small cramped study, packed to the ceiling with books, dust and half-finished ideas. I try to write something every day – either typing the actual stories on to my computer or jotting ideas down in a notebook that I always carry with me. I am not helped at all by my cat Sylvester, who is very good at parking his furry bottom on the exact spot where I am trying to write.

Date and place of birth:
27th October 1970
Bedford
Contact address:
22 Queens Crescent
St Albans
Hertfordshire AL4 9QQ

Selected titles

The Leap (Red Fox)

Buried Fire (Red Fox)

The Lost Treasure of Captain Blood (Walker Books)

The Viking Saga of Harri Bristlebeard (Walker Books)

Justin Credible's Word Play World (Walker Books)

Extract

As I hit the water, the warm sun was peeled off my back as if I had been flayed. My body stung with the cold, my ears rang with silence. All the little flitterings and soothing cries of that late summer day were left behind. I opened my eyes and saw around me a green-grey void. Behind me were the stones of the mill pool's edge, caked in long green fronds that stroked my legs with clammy tips.

I passed them by. Around and below was an emerald green emptiness, speared here and there by weak shafts of sunlight which had broken through the surface and now faded away into the depths. The pool was very deep.

Far off, in the green reaches, I saw Max. He was swimming, but swimming down …

From *The Leap* (Red Fox)

Favourite book: *The Lord of the Rings* by J.R.R. Tolkien comes close.
Favourite colour: Green
Favourite food: Fish and chips
Favourite word: Labyrinth
Favourite place: The Lake District
Where do your ideas come from? They are sparked off by places I visit, people I meet and feelings I've had; also by books of history and folklore. A lot of my ideas leap out at me on long walks.
What else might you have been? An archaeologist, searching for evidence of King Arthur.

Jonathan Stroud

Robert Swindells

I STARTED SCHOOL IN 1944: a year before the end of World War 2. I failed my 11 plus and left school at 15 with no qualifications of any sort. Now I have a master's degree and 60 published books. This shows that testing children proves *nothing*. I wrote my first novel as a thesis at teacher training college.

I have two grown-up daughters and three grandchildren. My eldest grandchild got two A* passes at GCSE, plus four As and three Bs. This shows either that he hasn't taken after his grandad, or that testing children proves *nothing*. I also have a wife, Brenda, who gained a BA (hons) in her 50s through the Open University, and who does everything else while I write. I couldn't function without her.

1 have no pets. There was a cat: a domestic longhair named Sappho, but Brenda and I travel a lot and Sappho was spending half her time in the cattery, so she went to live with a friend. I have learned that three things matter: peace, love and co-operation.

I like: misty mornings, Mozart, the Open University, vintage Bob Dylan, gazing into ponds, curry, Bradford City AFC, the life that I have. I dislike: bigots, DIY enthusiasts, violence, the motto *Don't get mad, get even* and the morons who quote it, the *Daily Express*.

Date and place of birth:
20th March 1939
Bradford
Contact address:
Reservoir Cats
4 Spring Row
Denholme Road
Oxenhope, Keighley
West Yorkshire BD22 9NR

Selected titles

Room 13 (Yearling Books)

Daz 4 Zoe (Puffin)

The Ice Palace (Puffin)

Hurricane Summer (Mammoth)

Stone Cold (Puffin)

Extract

You can call me Link.
It's not my name, but it's what I say when anybody asks, which isn't often. I'm invisible, see? One of the invisible people. Right now I'm sitting in a doorway watching the passers-by. They avoid looking at me. They're afraid I want something they've got, and they're right. Also, they don't want to think about me. They don't like reminding I exist. Me, and those like me. We're living proof that everything's not all right and we make the place untidy. Hang about and I'll tell you the story of my fascinating life.

From *Stone Cold* (Puffin)

Favourite book: *A Christmas Carol* by Charles Dickens
Favourite colour: Green
Favourite food: Lamb curry with roti
Favourite word: Peace
Favourite memory: Watching Bradford City win at Molyneaux to get into the Premiership (1999)
Where do your ideas come from? All the stories which I haven't written down yet are floating just above the heather on the Yorkshire Moors. They're invisible, but now and then when I'm walking up there I walk through one and breathe it in. When I get home there's a complete story inside my head which wasn't there when I set out.
What else might you have been? Before my first book was published I was a primary school teacher, so I suppose that's what I'd be now: unless I'd become an inspector, which strikes me as unlikely.

Nick Toczek

I WAS BROUGHT UP IN BRADFORD in West Yorkshire, and went to the grandly named Victoria Park Preparatory School and then to Bradford Grammar School, where I was fairly unpleasantly bullied by a couple of teachers (until I learned to fight back and be rebellious!) but also got on well with other teachers and with my fellow-pupils. I then went to Birmingham University and gained a degree in industrial metallurgy and so decided to become a poet (metal gets a bit boring!). My first published poems appeared in the school magazine and in the *Sunday Times* (!) for which I got paid!! I kept poetry notebooks (rather than diaries) in which I wrote almost every day. I still, more than thirty-five years later, stick to that rule of doing *some* creative writing *every day*.

I live in Bradford, but travel all over Britain as a poet, magician, story-teller and puppeteer. I usually work five or six days a week and travel up to 2,000 miles a week! I love it!!

I'm married to Gaynor and we've two teenage children, Matt and Becci. We've one gerbil and are thinking about getting a lizard. The attic of our house is huge. It's my office and where I usually write … although I also write in the loo and in front of the telly.

Date and place of birth:
20th September 1950
Shipley, Yorkshire
Contact address:
New House, 108 Ashgrove
Greengates, Bradford
West Yorkshire BD10 0BP
01274 610 275
slaphead@1000rpm.freeserve.
co.uk

Selected titles

The Dragon Who Ate Our School (Macmillan Children's Books)

Dragons Everywhere (Macmillan Children's Books)

Kick It! (Macmillan Children's Books)

Can Anybody be as Gloomy as Me? (Hodder Children's Books)

Never Stare at a Grizzly Bear (Macmillan Children's Books)

Extract

The day the dragon came to call
she ate the gate, the playground wall
and, slate by slate, the roof and all,
the staffroom, gym, and entrance hall.
And every classroom, big or small.

So …
She's undeniably great.
She's absolutely cool,
the dragon who ate
the dragon who ate
the dragon who ate our school.

Pupils panicked. Teachers ran.
She flew at them with wide wingspan.
She slew a few and then began
to chew through the lollipop man,
two parked cars and a transit van.

**From *The Dragon Who Ate Our School*
(Macmillan Children's Books)**

Favourite book: *The Little Girl Who Lives Down the Lane* by Niki Daly
Favourite colour: Red
Favourite food: Curries
Favourite word: Suddenly
Favourite place: Kettlewell, in the Yorkshire Dales
Where do your ideas come from? Words. I love written words, spoken words, strange words, foreign words etc. I love playing around with words, experimenting with how they fit together. I love the fact that one word, kicked around your head for a few minutes, can pick up other words and become a story, poem, joke, insult, idea, piece of journalism, etc.

John Rowe Townsend

I WROTE MY FIRST NOVEL (an adventure story) when I was 8 years old. It filled five red-backed notebooks (over 200 pages) and was illustrated in full colour, by me, in crayon. I had written poems before that, and I went on writing all through my schooldays. There was no stopping me.

But my first published book, *Gumble's Yard,* came much later, when I was working as a journalist. I wrote it partly because I felt existing books for children at that time were too harmless and hygienic, not dealing with the realities of life. (It wouldn't be true now.) But mostly I wrote it because it was inside me, hollering to get out.

I have three children, now grown up, and once had a cat called Modesty, who was VERY CLEVER. The children are called Thea, Nicholas and Penny. And I have seven grandchildren, but I'm running out of space.

Date and place of birth:
10th May 1922
Leeds
Contact address:
Oxford University Press
Children's Publicity
Great Clarendon Street
Oxford OX2 6DP

Selected titles

Gumble's Yard (OUP)

The Intruder (OUP)

Tom Tiddler's Ground (CUP)

The Islanders (Red Fox)

Noah's Castle (Green Bay)

Extract

Arnold, a north-country boy, has the job of guiding a strange, unknown man across the dangerous sands of an estuary. Halfway across, the man asks him his name and he replies, "Arnold Haithwaite".

They walked on for two or three minutes in silence. Arnold prodded the sand from time to time. There weren't any quicksands here, but the texture helped him to tell where the tide had got to.

"Don't be scared if it's round your feet in a few minutes," he said. "I told you you'd get your shoes wet." But now it was the stranger who didn't seem to be listening. He plodded on with his head down.
"You're all right, are you?" asked Arnold after a minute or two.
"Oh yes, I'm all right. *What* did you say your name was?"
"Arnold Haithwaite," said Arnold again.
The man stood still
"Come here!" he said.
Arnold went close to him. It was dark now. The stranger pulled a flashlight from his raincoat pocket and shone it suddenly in Arnold's face, making him blink.
"You can't be Arnold Haithwaite," he said. "Because *I'm* Arnold Haithwaite."
From *The Intruder* (OUP)

Favourite book: *The Wind in the Willows* by Kenneth Grahame
Favourite colour: Blue
Favourite food: Fish (especially swordfish if I can afford it)
Favourite word: Cellar-door (because it sounds so lovely)
Favourite place: Cambridge, where I live
Where do your ideas come from? Ideas come from anywhere: people I've met, problems that have made me think, snatches of conversation overheard, something I've read in the newspaper. The world is teeming with ideas. The problem is to find the idea that's right for me.
What else might you have been? A disappointed would-be writer.

John Rowe Townsend

Hazel Townson

MY FIRST POEM WAS PUBLISHED in a local paper when I was 9. I then wrote two plays which were performed in high school (at age 14–15).

I began contributing to *Punch* whilst a student and wrote regularly for them for many years (verse and short articles). This was great fun.

Whilst working as a young people's services librarian I found many children struggling with the fiction books they had borrowed and I decided to supply more manageable books, shorter, fast-moving and humorous. I couldn't find many to buy for my libraries, so I began writing some myself.

I'm now a full-time writer, working in a spare bedroom at home, and I spend much time in schools helping children with their creative writing and hoping they will help me with mine. My favourite authors as a child were Beatrix Potter and Richmal Crompton and I'd love to think my books might give as much pleasure as theirs gave me.

Date and place of birth:
12th April
Nelson, Lancashire
Contact address:
53 Prestwich Hills
Prestwich
Manchester M25 9PY

Selected titles

The Speckled Panic (Andersen Press)

Your Dad, My Mum (Andersen Press/Red Fox)

Disaster Bag (Andersen Press)

Terrible Tuesday – picture book (Andersen Press)

The Deathwood Letters (Andersen Press/Red Fox)

Extract

Although my waist is badly-placed
And not so very slender,
Although my hips have strained their zips
And snapped a back suspender;
Although my feet are far from neat,
My calves are second-grade,
In spite of this I never miss
A mannequin parade.
I love to gape at style and shape
In growing sweet confusion
'Til they have twined about my mind
A one-with-them illusion.
And I may buy what takes my eye,
Convinced that I can wear it.
For those with hips to strain their zips
Have lips to grin and bear it.

**From 'Hypnotic Fit' (written for *Punch*
after a visit to a mannequin parade)**

Favourite book: *The Winter of the Birds* by Helen Cresswell
Favourite colour: Lavender
Favourite food: Swordfish and strawberries (but not together!)
Favourite word: Peace
Favourite place: Lancashire's lovely Pendle Valley where I spent a very happy childhood.
Where do your ideas come from? The news, especially local news; overheard bits of conversation; remembering my own childhood; being generally observant; and completely out of the blue!
What else might you have been? A bookshop proprietor in a quiet spot somewhere near the sea, with just enough customers to keep me solvent but also plenty of time to read the stock.

Kaye Umansky

I WAS AN ONLY CHILD, growing up in Plymstock, near Plymouth in Devon. Mum was a music teacher, Dad was retired. I spent a lot of time reading and writing stories to amuse myself. Mum put me in for every exam and music festival going. I wasn't crazy about school, apart from singing in the choir and acting in the annual play. I loved English lessons and hated PE and maths.

We always had cats when I was growing up. I have two now.

The books I read as a child were William and Jennings stories, *The Swish of the Curtain* (Pamela Brown), *Ballet Shoes* (Noel Streatfeild), *The Hobbit* and everything by E. Nesbit. I loved funny books and devoured anything with magic in it.

Things I loved (and still do) include sunshine, snow, holidays in hot countries, listening to music, and cats. Things I hated (and still do) include bullies, kidneys, running, skin on rice pudding, heights, crocodiles, and biros that leak in your handbag.

Date and place of birth:
6th December 1946
Plymouth, Devon
Contact address:
Jan Powling
Speaking of Books
9 Guildford Grove
Greenwich
London SE10 8JY

Selected titles

Pongwiffy – A Witch of Dirty Habits (Puffin)

Wilma's Wicked Revenge (Puffin)

Three Singing Pigs (A & C Black)

Need a Swim, Jim (Bodley Head)

Hammy House of Horror (Hodder Children's Books)

Favourite book: *The Swish of the Curtain* by Pamela Brown
Favourite colour: Red
Favourite food: Cheese
Favourite word: Moonbeam
Favourite memory: Seeing my baby daughter Ella for the first time
Where do your ideas come from? Listening to people's conversations and observing what they do; things I have read, dreams and daydreams.
What else might you have been? A trapeze artist in a circus. Being terrified of heights, I admire them hugely. Also a professional singer. I sang with a band for years, but wasn't good enough to make it my living.

K E Umansky

Extract

Lost in Woolworths

Oh no! I'm lost in Woolworths!
My mum's nowhere in sight!
She was buying me new trainers
(my old ones are too tight).

She was over by the checkout.
I was at the Pick 'N' Mix,
But now she's gone and vanished
And I'm in an awful fix.

Oh, the panic! Oh, the horror!
Oh, the heat, the noise, the crowd!
I think I might start crying
And I think I might be loud!

WAAAAAAAAAAAAHHHH!

Then, suddenly, I see her
With my trainers in a packet.
"Oh, there you are! Where have you been?
And what's that awful racket?"

I take her hand. I smile a bit.
She buys me Juicy Fruits,
And everything's all right again
'Til I get lost in Boots.

From *Here Come the Heebie-Jeebies and Other Scary Poems* (Hodder Children's Books)

Jean Ure

I STARTED WRITING WHEN I WAS 6 YEARS OLD and had my first book published while I was still at school. These are some of the books I loved as a child: *Winnie-the-Pooh*, *Little Women*, *A Little Princess*, and the 'Just William' books.

I live in a 300-year-old house with my husband and our family of rescued animals – four cats and seven dogs. I love: animals, music, avacado pears and raw carrots. I hate: cruelty. I work in my study, surrounded by all the animals. Here is a secret: four of the dogs sleep in bed with us! This is not a secret: I am a vegetarian. I do not eat animals!

Date and place of birth:
Caterham, Surrey
New Year's Day, some
time ago
Contact address:
88 Southbridge Road
Croydon
CR0 1AF
020 8760 9818
Fax: 020 8688 6565

Selected titles

Skinny Melon and Me

Becky Bananas

Fruit and Nutcase

Shrinking Violet

Big Tom

All published by HarperCollins

Extract

My dad's an Elvis Prestley look-alike. He's got a white suit just like Elvis had, and a guitar, and he sings all the songs that Elvis sang. *Blue Suede Shoes*, *Hound Dog*, *Love me Tender*, *Love me True*. He knows them all!
I've drawn a picture of my dad being Elvis on my bedroom wall. I'll draw it again, now.
I'm always drawing on my bedroom wall. When I've filled up all the space I'm going to start on the ceiling. I'll be taller by then. I'll stand on a stepladder and I'll be able to reach.

From *Fruit and Nutcase* (HarperCollins)

Favourite book: *Little Women* by Louisa M. Alcott
Favourite colour: Blue
Favourite food: Avocado pear
Favourite word: Kindness
Favourite place: Home
Where do your ideas come from? All over! But especially from memories of being young, things I see and hear, my imagination and other people's books.
What else might you have been? When I was younger I would have said a dancer. Now I would say, "I would work with animals."

Jean Ure

Martin Waddell

MY FIRST SCHOOL WAS MISS LOGAN'S in Newcastle, Co. Down, and that was good fun.

I always played football – in fact I played almost every game there was! Then were always stories too – stories of the Norse myths and a lovely story called *Elizabeth the Cow Ghost*. I still have that book.

I still live in Newcastle in Co. Down – my parents brought me here when I was a few days old because the Blitz was happening in Belfast. I live in an old house that looks out over Dandrum Bay and I work in a converted stone barn at the side of the house. It's wonderful and I love it!

Date and place of birth:
10th April 1941
Belfast
Northern Ireland
Contact address:
David Higham Associates
5–8 Lower John Street
London W1R 4HA

Selected titles

Can't You Sleep, Little Bear? – picture book (Walker Books)

Owl Babies – picture book (Walker Books)

The Ghost in the Blue Velvet Dress – for 8–12 years (Walker Books)

The Ghost and Bertie Boggin – for 7–10 years (Walker Books)

The Orchard Book of Ghostly Stories (Orchard Books)

Extract

There once was a duck
who had the bad luck to live
with a lazy old farmer.
The duck did the work.
The farmer stayed
all day in bed.

From *Farmer Duck* (Walker Books)

Favourite book: *Treasure Island* by R.L. Stevenson
Favourite colour: Red
Favourite food: Steak and chips
Favourite word: Lots of favourites
Favourite place: Newcastle, Co. Down – a seaside town at the foot of the mountains of Mourne.
Where do your ideas come from? Everywhere!

I hear people talking, I hear children playing and squabbling. I see a lovely picture or I see a sad picture or a funny picture.
What else might you have been? Perhaps a footballer! I've been a writer for so long that it's very difficult to imagine being anything else.

Nick Warburton

I WAS BORN AND BROUGHT UP IN WOODFORD, east of London. We had our holidays in Norfolk, where my mum used to live. Nelson used to live round there, too, but long before my time.

Once I knew what a writer was, I wanted to be one. Writers, however, don't have "proper jobs" so I never said that that's what I wanted to do. I said I wanted to be a policeman or a journalist, and I trained to be a teacher. When I was 33, I decided to stop teaching. I've been writing now for more than 20 years – sometimes books, sometimes plays for stage, radio and television.

I live in Cambridge and I have a small office in town. I have three cats who keep an eye on the house while I'm busy writing and my wife is even busier teaching. I don't have many dislikes, apart from tomatoes, sprouts and telephones. I love cricket, and reading and acting. I always enjoy pretending to be someone else, someone who shouts a bit more than I do.

I remember reading a thrilling book about sailing ships when I was 10. Unfortunately I can't remember what it was called or who wrote it. After that I read a lot of Dickens – I still do. I still love stories about the sea, too.

Date and place of birth:
2nd February 1947
Woodford, Essex
Contact address:
David Higham Associates
5–8 Lower John Street
Golden Square
London WIF 9HA
nickwarbur@aol.com

Selected titles

Lost in Africa (Walker Books)

War Record (OUP)

Ackford's Monster (Walker Books)

Gladiators Never Blink (Walker Books)

The Strange Change of Flora Young (Walker Books)

Extract

So Flora crawled under a web of twisted music stands, between the dry tight skins of the old drums, guided by the bobbing beam of Mr Todd's torch. She reached out, felt the brick corner with her fingers and stood up. It wasn't easy – the alcove was hardly bigger than a sentry-box. A pair of old scales and a wonky pile of dog-eared books hemmed her in. There was no tea-chest.

Before edging her way back, she picked up one of the books from the pile and looked at it. Mental Arithmetic it said on the cover. She flicked it open. It wasn't much of a thing to do. But it was enough.

A little cloud of specks danced in the torch beam and she saw pages of pounds, shillings and pence in neat columns.

From *The Strange Change of Flora Young* (Walker Books)

Favourite book: So hard to choose! *Bleak House* by Charles Dickens
Favourite colour: Green
Favourite food: Sausage and mash
Favourite word: Abundance
Favourite place: Chichester, where I went to college and made so many friends
Where do your ideas come from? My ideas come from all over the place. Day-dreaming and listening to people telling me stories about themselves or their families. I listen to strangers, too, talking in shops or on trains.
What else might you have been? Well, I was a teacher and I enjoyed that. I would have liked to be an actor, though, or a director. But I can't imagine not writing. It's a hobby and a job.

Colin West

I WAS BROUGHT UP IN THE 1950s, and the books I remember enjoying most of all were Alison Uttley's 'Little Grey Rabbit' stories, Edward Lear's nonsense verse and the Rupert Bear annuals. I also loved the pictures in these books, and made my own versions in little notebooks.

I also soaked up all the songs of the time. There were funny ones like 'My Old Man's a Dustman', and dreamy ones like 'Stranger in Paradise'. I also remember the advertising slogans, such as the very clever 'Drinka Pinta Milka Day'. All these things made me want to write too. I left school as soon as I could, to go to art college, where I began writing stories and poems which I could illustrate myself. It's great fun, so I've been doing it ever since!

I now live in a house which is about a hundred years old, and which was once a laundry. It's got big windows (a bit like an old village school) and the attic has nice wood panelling. I work in a room up there, and look out on to the garden, where I can see birds drinking from my bird bath (or splashing about in it). I still love art and music, and most of all collecting old books.

Date and place of birth:
21st May 1951
Epping
Contact address:
14 High Street
Epping
Essex CM16 4AB

Selected titles

Monty, the Dog who Wears Glasses (Collins)

The Big Book of Nonsense (Hutchinson Children's Books)

One Day in the Jungle (Walker Books)

Mr Potts the Potty Teacher (A & C Black)

Have You Seen the Crocodile? (Walker Books)

Illustration

What do Teachers Dream of?

What do teachers dream of,
In mountains and in lowlands?
They dream of exclamation marks,
Full stops and semi-colons!

***From The Big Book of Nonsense* (Hutchinson Children's Books)**

Favourite book: The Bible
Favourite colour: Yellow
Favourite food: Cheeseburger
Favourite word: Finished! (when said by my dentist)
Favourite place: My living room, with the sun shining in, a nice CD playing and a good book in my hand.
Where do your ideas come from? My ideas seem to come when I'm in a relaxed state of mind – just before nodding off to sleep, resting whilst listening to music or soaking in the bath! It also helps to draw characters – it makes them more real, and can spark off fresh ideas.
What else might you have been? I've always wanted to be an artist of some sort, so I never considered anything else. However, I do envy people who are musically gifted, and I would have loved to have been a jazz pianist.

Colin West

Brian Wildsmith

MY SCHOOL DAYS WERE VERY HAPPY DAYS. At primary school, we all knew our alphabet at 4½ years old, could write at 5 and at 6 years old were reading wonderful stories from Greek classics (but not in Greek). Looking back, I was a good student in all subjects except French. My French teacher told me I was the worst student she had ever had. I now live in France and I still have difficulty with the language. I loved sport, in particular cricket. I adored the game, became school captain and later played at university.

My entry into the art world remains a mystery to me. Poor but loving parents of four children, who made us believe that we could achieve anything if we gave everything to it, were a major factor. It was wartime, paints were unobtainable, but pencils and paper were available. I didn't think I was very good at drawing, but my old friends tell me I drew the best racing cars and airplane dogfights in the school.

At the age of 16 on my way to a chemistry class, I had a moment of revelation, a burning desire to create. I left school that day and enrolled at the local art school.

I now live in a very beautiful village and my studio overlooks the Mediterranean Sea in southern France. My studio is a complete mess and I spend half my time trying to find my paints and paintbrushes.

Date and place of birth:
22nd January 1930
Penistone, South Yorkshire,
Contact address:
Oxford University Press
Children's Publicity
Great Clarendon Street
Oxford OX2 6DP

Selected titles

A B C (Star Bright Books)   *The Hunter and his Dog* (OUP)

Carousel (OUP)   *Professor Noah's Spaceship* (OUP)

Joseph (OUP)

Illustration

From *Mary* (OUP)

Favourite colour: I love ALL colours
Favourite food: Fish and chips
Favourite word: Love
Favourite place: Castellaras, France
Where do your ideas come from? My ideas come from watching people, birds, animals and the glorious world in which we live. Here is how *The Hunter and his Dog* started.
Many years ago we had a beloved little dog. His name was Vanic. When he was 4 years old he became ill. He became blind, and then lost his sense of smell. Next door to us lived a huge ferocious dog – Boss Dog of the village he was. Everyone was terrified of him. His name was Sheriff. When Vanic became ill, Sheriff appeared every day at 6am at our front door, howling until we let him into the house. He then sat beside Vanic and licked him *all* day, trying to cure the little dog. I then realised that animals do have the gift of compassion and this became the basis of my picture book.
What else might you have been? I like to think I would have made it as a concert pianist – failing that a scientist.

Brian Wildsmith

Jacqueline Wilson

I LOVED WRITING STORIES when I was at school – and I also liked Art. I was useless at Maths and P.E. I always wanted to be a writer and was lucky enough to get my first short story published when I was 17. I've now written about 70 books!

I have one lovely grown-up daughter, Emma. I don't have any pets as I travel around too much and it wouldn't be fair. I like to write my stories in longhand in notebooks – and then type them out on my computer. I'm not very good at using computers – I can't work modern machines!

I've got a little study but I'm happy to work anywhere. I often write my stories on trains.

I liked reading family stories when I was a child. Reading is still my favourite hobby. I also like going to art galleries and films, shopping, swimming and dancing.

Date and place of birth:
17th December
Bath
Contact address:
Transworld Children's Books
61–63 Uxbridge Road
London W5 5SA
www.jacquelinewilson.co.uk

Selected titles

Double Act

The Story of Tracy Beaker

The Illustrated Mum

The Suitcase Kid

Cliffhanger

All published by Yearling Books

Extract

We're twins. I'm Ruby. She's Garnet. We're identical. There's very few people who can tell us apart. Well, until we start talking. I tend to go on and on. Garnet is much quieter.

That's because I can't get a word in edgeways.

We are exactly the same height and weight. I eat a bit more than Garnet. I love sweets, and I like salty things too. I once ate thirteen packets of crisps in one day.

From *Double Act* (Yearling Books)

Favourite book: *Nancy and Plum* by Betty MacDonald
Favourite colour: Black … and I like silver too
Favourite food: Fruit (but I also love cream doughnuts!)
Favourite word: Rainbow
Favourite place: My favourite place is Boston in America – I go there once or twice a year with my daughter Emma.

Where do your ideas come from? I don't really know where my ideas come from – it's a bit like asking you where your dreams come from. They just pop into my head!
What else might you have been? I would have worked in a second-hand bookshop. I have 15,000 books crammed into my tiny house so I could start up my own shop now!

Jacqueline Wilson

Benjamin Zephaniah

MY FULL NAME IS Benjamin Obadiah Iqbal Zephaniah, which is Christian, Jewish and Muslim. My poetry is strongly influenced by the music and poetry of Jamaica and I can't remember a time when I was not creating poetry. I wanted to reach as many people as possible so my mission was to take poetry everywhere and I was able to do this through performing my poems directly to people and using television and radio.

I try to write poems that are fun but they should also have a serious message. I am very concerned about racism, animal rights and pollution and I have always believed that boys and girls should be treated equally. I hate wars and I think it is not right that adults should tell children not to deal with disputes by fighting and then those same adults go and fight in wars. I think armies should be banned.

Most of my best friends are animals and I am passionate about being vegan. I love jogging, kung-fu, football, collecting old banknotes and kissing.

Date and place of birth:
No one is sure of my exact date of birth; rumour has it either 15th April or 15th March 1958, Birmingham
Contact address:
PO Box 673
East Ham
London E6 3QD
www.benjamin
zephaniah.com

Selected titles

Wicked World – poetry (Puffin)

Refugee Boy – novel (Bloomsbury Children's Books)

Face – novel (Bloomsbury Children's Books)

Talking Turkeys – poetry (Puffin)

Funky Chickens – poetry (Puffin)

Extract

Who's Who

I used to think nurses
Were women,
I used to think police
Were men,
I used to think poets
Were boring,
Until I became one of them.

From *Talking Turkeys* (Puffin)

Favourite book: *A Book of Nonsense* by Mervyn Peake
Favourite colour: Red
Favourite food: Butterbeans
Favourite word: Overstanding
Where do your ideas come from? I look everywhere for ideas. I read a lot about things that are happening in the world. I read lots of newspapers from other countries. I watch the news a lot, and I argue with people to hear their points of view. I also spend a lot of time listening to what people are saying on buses, in shops and on aeroplanes, and most importantly, I spend an awful lot of time listening to myself.
What else might you have been? A kung-fu teacher. It's the only thing I ever qualified in. I used to run my own school but poetry took over so I now teach needy friends.

Benjamin Zephaniah

1. How to Use this Book

The Uses of Stories

By introducing children to a rich range of written and illustrated material you will:

- make stories more important and enjoyable for them

- encourage them to read with confidence, using techniques such as timing, expression, tone of voice, accent and intonation

- enable them to talk with confidence about literature

- encourage them to listen attentively in a range of contexts

- help them to develop an ear for language

- stimulate their own spoken language, equipping them with the skills to speak with clarity, confidence and expression

- help them to learn about the features of good-quality writing and understand how successful stories work

- foster their voluntary independent reading.

The Reading Adult

Research has revealed again and again that the impact of an adult, such as a parent or teacher, on children's book choices and on their language development is considerable. The two most important factors in fostering children's reading are teacher influence and the provision of a wide range of material. So, teachers must be readers themselves. There is no short cut, no easy answer, no definitive booklist. We need to have read the books we present to children, we need to select them with care and knowledge and to be skilled in judging when and how to use them. I find that keeping up with the plethora of material available can be time consuming and demanding, but it is also highly enjoyable and rewarding.

All interested professionals can keep up with their reading in some of the ways explored below.

1. Having close and regular contact with the Schools Library Service
The librarians advise on and recommend titles; organise courses and conferences, workshops and book reviewing groups; and produce fiction, poetry and non-fiction lists. Teachers might try to visit their Schools Library Service HQ on a regular basis and depart with a small collection of books: a couple of picture books, a poetry collection, a short story anthology, some recently published non-fiction texts, perhaps a controversial children's story about which the librarian wants an opinion and one or two books the librarian feels they might enjoy. Some Schools Library Services may arrange book loans that

can be delivered to schools on request. Also the mobile library may be able to visit your school regularly.

2. Keeping in close and regular contact with a good bookshop
Suppliers who specialise in children's literature – like Sonia Benster of The Children's Bookshop, 37–39 Lidget Street, Lindley, Huddersfield HD3 3JF; and Madeleine Lindley of The Book Centre, Unit 20, Broadgate, Broadway Business Park, Chadderton, Oldham, Lancashire OL9 9XA – are widely read and select books with knowledge and care. They will send material, recommend titles, and tell their customers what new publications have come on the market and which are the most popular with children. They also will attend teachers' courses and parents' evenings to mount displays and sell books. The Country Bookshop Ltd, Hassop Station, Bakewell, Derbyshire DE45 1NW (e-mail: info@country bookshop.co.uk) is an on-line bookstore with over 15,000 titles in stock and 1.5 million titles listed. You can search by title, author or key word, browse numerous categories, including author information, and place orders on-line not only for titles in print in the United Kingdom but for those published in the United States. The store can also do a search for out-of-print titles.

3. Becoming a member of the Reading and Language Information Centre
The centre is based at the University of Reading. Members automatically receive new books every term, have free access to the permanent display of 15,000 children's books and resources and receive a discount on past publications. These include *Practical Ways to Organise Reading, Fiction in the Literacy Hour, Children Making Books, Individualised Reading, Storytelling in Schools, How Schools Teach Reading, Helping Your Child with Reading* and *Reading IT*. The centre has an e-mail address (reading-centre@reading.ac.uk) and a web site (www.ralic.reading. ac.uk) for updates and further information.

4. Reading the reviews in journals
These include those produced by the Thimble Press and *Child Education*. The bookseller Waterstones produces an excellent *Guide to Children's Books*, an annotated booklist in which the very best of classic and contemporary fiction books for children are reviewed.

5. Becoming a member of the School Library Association
The School Library Association (SLA) is at Unit 2, Lotmead Business Village, Lotmead Farm, Wanborough, Swindon SN4 0UY. It provides a range of published guidelines and booklists; a quarterly journal, *The School Librarian*, with articles and book reviews and CD-ROMS; local and national training courses; a network of local branches; a help-line for members; and an advisory and information service.

6. Visiting one of the national exhibitions
Educational Exhibitions Ltd, 14 Gainsborough Road, London N12 8AG, organise a comprehensive range of exhibitions that take place throughout the country and include the North of England Conference and Exhibition, the British Education Training and Technology (BETT) Show at Olympia, the National Association for the Teaching of English (NATE) Annual Conference, the Education Show at the Birmingham NEC, the Wales Education Conference and the North West Regional Conference and Exhibition. All the major

publishers are represented at these exhibitions and you can view the recently published books, materials and reading resources.

7. Listening to children and finding out what they enjoy reading
The stories children enjoy depend on a number of factors: age and maturity, ability, environment, experience and interests, even the mood they are in at a particular time. Like adults, children have preferences and a story that one child will read avidly may have little impact on another.

The Reading Entitlement

The National Literacy Strategy Framework sets out clearly the teaching objectives for Reception to Year 6 and outlines the kinds of stories, poems, plays and non-fiction texts children should encounter as they progress through the primary years. Central to the framework is the Literacy Hour, a dedicated time each day in which the teacher develops children's reading skills through instruction, questioning, eliciting responses and refining and extending children's contributions. The Literacy Hour is not, however, about going through a minimum of texts in maximum, pleasure-destroying detail, interrogating the writing in such a way that children are turned off books and reading. It is about developing in children a love of reading by using a wide range of really interesting and challenging books and dealing with these books in a sensitive way. This material should include the following.

POETRY
Playground Chants
Nursery Rhymes
Miniature Poems
Simple Counting Rhymes
Action Verse
Syllabic Poetry
Songs and Lyrics
Rhythmic Verse
Haikus
Rhyming Couplets
Clerihews
Tankas
Patterned Poems
Kennings
Cinquains
Humorous Verse
Free Verse
Performance Poetry
Tongue-twisters
Prayers
Conversation Poems
Alphabet Poems
Riddles
Narrative Poetry
Limericks
Shape/Concrete Poems
Ballads
Choral Verse
Acrostics
Epitaphs

PROSE
Nursery Tales
Folk Tales
Traditional Stories
Wonder Tales
Fairy Tales
Stories with Familiar Settings
Tall Stories
Anecdotes
Family History Stories
Jokes
Tongue-twisters
Puns
Word Puzzles
Warning Tales
Fables
Myths
Legends
Sagas
Parables
Dilemma Stories
Stories from Different Cultures
School Stories
Historical Stories
Science Fiction
Ghost Stories
Mystery Stories
Humorous Stories
Fantasy Stories
Monologues
Adventure Stories

NON-FICTION
Simple Non-fiction Texts
Simple Instructions
Information Texts
Signs
Simple Dictionaries
Glossaries
Labels
Recounts of Events
Indexes
Captions
Recounts of Visits
Thesauruses
Lists
Non-chronological Reports
Explanations
Letters
Encyclopaedias
Articles
Newspapers
Magazines
Advertisements
Circulars
Flyers
Discussion Texts
Debates
Editorials
Leaflets
Rules
Recipes
Directions
Commentaries
Diaries
Journals
Biographies
Autobiographies
Anecdotes
Reference Texts
Discussion Texts
Public Documents

The books recommended below are those which many children have read and enjoyed, and in some measure represent the great variety of reading material now available. The selection is chosen so that the majority of the authors can be found in *The Address Book*.

Suggested texts

- TEN PICTURE BOOKS
  The Baby who Wouldn't Go to Bed by Helen Cooper, Doubleday/Picture Corgi
  The Big Big Sea by Martin Waddell, illustrated by Jennifer Eachus, Walker Books
  Flora's Blanket by Debi Gliori, Orchard Books
  The Hoppameleon by Paul Geraghty, Hutchinson Children's Books
  Jaguar by Helen Cowcher, Scholastic Children's Books/Milet Ltd
  Nicky by Tony and Zoë Ross, Andersen Press
  My Cat Cuddles by Gervase Phinn, Child's Play International
  Picture Book by Ian Beck, Scholastic Children's Books
  This is the Bear by Sarah Hayes, illustrated by Helen Craig, Walker Books
  Walk with the Wolf by Janni Howker, illustrated by Sarah Fox-Davies, Walker Books

- TEN NOVELTY AND POP-UP BOOKS
  Aesop's Funky Fables by Vivian French, illustrated by Korky Paul, Puffin
  The Animal Orchestra by Nick Sharratt, Walker Books
  Brian Wildsmith's ABC by Brian Wildsmith, Star Bright Books
  Cheese and Tomato Spider by Nick Sharratt, Scholastic Children's Books/ Hippo
  Fancy That! by Jan Pieńkowski, Orchard Books
  Haunted House by Jan Pieńkowski, Walker Books
  Noah's Ark, illustrated by Jane Ray, Orchard Books
  The Very Busy Spider by Eric Carle, Hamish Hamilton
  The Very Hungry Caterpillar by Eric Carle, Puffin
  The Very Lonely Firefly by Eric Carle, Philomel Books

- TEN FOLK AND FAIRY TALE COLLECTIONS
  Alan Garner's Book of British Fairy Tales by Alan Garner, Collins
  Beastly Tales from Here and There by Vikram Seth, Phoenix
  Collins Treasury of Fairy Tales, edited by Helen Cresswell, Picture Lions
  Enchantment by Kevin Crossley-Holland, Orion
  Fairy Tales retold by Berlie Doherty, illustrated by Jane Ray, Walker Books
  Goldilocks and the Three Bears by Tony Mitton, Walker Books
  Tales of Wonder and Magic collected by Berlie Doherty, Walker Books
  The Three Indian Princesses by Jamila Gavin, Mammoth
  Thumbelina, retold by Jenny Nimmo, Macdonald Young Books
  The Young Oxford Book of Folk Tales by Kevin Crossley-Holland, OUP

- TEN BIG BOOKS
  All Fall Down by Brian Wildsmith, OUP
  Can't you Sleep, Little Bear? by Martin Waddell, illustrated by Barbara Firth, Walker Books
  A Dark, Dark Tale by Ruth Brown, Andersen Press/Red Fox
  The Fish who Could Wish by John Bush, illustrated by Korky Paul, OUP

The House Cat by Helen Cooper, Scholastic Children's Books
The Hunter by Paul Geraghty, Hutchinson's Children's Books/Red Fox
Kangaroos by Martin Waddell, Ginn
Pig in the Pond by Martin Waddell, illustrated by Jill Barton, Walker Books
The Snow Lambs by Debi Gliori, Scholastic Children's Books
Titch by Pat Hutchins, Red Fox

● TEN STORY BOOKS FOR YOUNGER READERS
The Butterfly Lion by Michael Morpurgo, Collins
Juggler by Peter Dixon, Barrington Stoke
Little Soldier by Bernard Ashley, Orchard Books
Lizzie Dripping by Helen Cresswell, Puffin
A Necklace of Raindrops and Other Stories by Joan Aiken, Crown Publishing
  Group
Only a Show by Anne Fine, Puffin
Ronnie and the Giant Millipede by Jenny Nimmo, Walker Books
Silly Sons and Dozy Daughters by Rose Impey, Orchard Books
Sophie in the Saddle by Dick King-Smith, Walker Books
Who's Talking? by Jean Ure, Orchard Books.

● TEN COLLECTIONS OF MYTHS AND LEGENDS
Green Boy by Susan Cooper, Bodley Head/Puffin
The Midas Touch by Jan Mark, Walker Books
Myths and Legends by Anthony Horowitz, Kingsfisher
100 World Myths and Legends by Geraldine McCaughrean, Dolphin
One Thousand and One Arabian Nights by Geraldine McCaughrean, OUP
The Orchard Book of Egyptian Gods and Pharoahs by Robert Swindells,
  Orchard Books
The Orchard Book of Greek Myths by Geraldine McCaughrean, Orchard Books
The Orchard Book of Mythical Birds and Beasts by Margaret Mayo,
  illustrated by Jane Ray, Orchard Books
Robin of Sherwood by Michael Morpurgo, Hodder Children's Books
The Story Giant by Brian Patten, HarperCollins
The Story of Creation illustrated by Jane Ray, Orchard Books

● TEN CLASSIC NOVELS FOR OLDER READERS
The Adventures of Tom Sawyer by Mark Twain, Penguin
Alice in Wonderland by Lewis Carroll, Puffin
Black Beauty by Anna Sewell, Penguin
Little Women by Louisa M. Alcott, Pavilion
Moonfleet by J.M. Faulkner, Penguin
Peter Pan by J.M. Barrie, Penguin
The Railway Children by E. Nesbit, Penguin
The Secret Garden by Frances Hodgson Burnett, Puffin
Swallows and Amazons by Arthur Ransome, Red Fox
The Wind in the Willows by Kenneth Grahame, Penguin

● TEN SHORT STORY COLLECTIONS FOR OLDER READERS
Apricots at Midnight by Adèle Geras, Atheneum
Badger on the Barge by Janni Howker, Walker Books
Britannia: 100 Great Stories from British History by Geraldine McCaughrean,
  Orion Children's Books

Dockside School Stories by Bernard Ashley, Walker Books
School Stories, chosen by Jan Mark, Kingfisher
Smart Girls by Robert Leeson, Walker Books
The Orchard Book of Ghostly Stories by Martin Waddell, Orchard Books
The Walker Book of Animal Stories by Michael Rosen, Jan Mark and Dick King-Smith, Walker Books
The Walker Book of Funny Stories by Brian Patten, Ann Pilling and Ann Jungman, Walker Books
The Walker Book of Magical Stories by Vivian French, Sarah Hayes and Martin Waddell, Walker Books

- TWELVE NOVELS FOR OLDER READERS IN DIFFERENT GENRES
  Aquarius Divide by Jan Mark, Viking (science fiction)
  The Boggart by Susan Cooper, Bodley Head/Puffin (fantasy)
  Chewing the Cud by Dick King-Smith, Puffin (autobiography)
  Children of Winter by Berlie Doherty, Mammoth (historical story)
  The Dark behind the Curtain by Gillian Cross, Scholastic Point (mystery story)
  The Ghost of Thomas Kempe by Penelope Lively, Egmont (ghost story)
  Hurricane Summer by Robert Swindells, Mammoth (war story)
  Madame Doubtfire by Anne Fine, Puffin (family story)
  Megastars: Skateboard Secret by Michael Hardcastle, Magnet (sport story)
  The Sheep-Pig by Dick King-Smith, Puffin (animal story)
  Spilling the Beans on Marie-Antoinette by Alec Smart, Miles Kelly Publishing (biography)
  The White Horse Gang by Nina Bawden, Gollancz (adventure story)

- TEN PLAYS
  Bill's New Frock: The Play by Anne Fine, Longman
  Carrie's War by Nina Bawden, OUP
  The Curse of the Egyptian Mummy by Pat Hutchins, Samuel French
  The Demon Headmaster by Gillian Cross, OUP
  The Fwog Pwince: The Twuth! by Kaye Umansky, Longman
  Mystery at Winklesea by Helen Cresswell, Ward Lock
  PERCI and Other Plays by Gervase Phinn, Longman
  The Turbulent Term of Tyke Tyler by Gene Kemp, OUP
  Shakespeare Stories by Leon Garfield, OUP
  Stranger Danger? by Anne Fine, Ginn

- TEN POETRY ANTHOLOGIES
  Because a Fire was in my Head, edited by Michael Morpurgo, Faber
  The Kingfisher Book of Comic Verse, chosen by Roger McGough, Kingfisher
  Mother gave a Shout: Poems by Women and Children, edited by Susanna Steele and Morag Styles, Volcano Press
  100 Best Poems for Children, edited by Roger McGough, Viking
  The Orchard Book of Poems, chosen by Adrian Mitchell, Orchard Books
  A Poem for Everyone, collected by Michael Harrison and Christopher Stuart-Clark, OUP
  The Puffin Book of 20th Century Children's Verse, edited by Brian Patten, Puffin
  Scottish Poems, chosen by John Rice, Macmillan
  Wordwhirls and other Shape Poems, collected by John Foster, OUP

A Year full of Poems, edited by Michael Harrison and Christopher Stuart-Clark, OUP

- TEN INDIVIDUAL POETRY COLLECTIONS
  Bad Bad Cats by Roger McGough, Puffin
  Barking Back at Dogs by Brian Moses, Macmillan
  Big Billy by Peter Dixon, P. Dixon Press
  The Day our Teacher went Batty, by Gervase Phinn, Puffin
  Plum by Tony Mitton, Scholastic Children's Books
  The River Girl by Wendy Cope, Faber
  Smile, Please! by Tony Bradman, Puffin
  Talking Turkeys by Benjamin Zephaniah, Puffin
  Thawing Frozen Frogs by Brian Patten, Puffin
  Two's Company by Jackie Kay, Puffin

- TEN NON-FICTION BOOKS
  The Book about Books by Chris Powling, A & C Black
  The Children's Illustrated Bible, retold by Selina Hastings, Dorling Kindersley
  Come Home with Us, Oxfam/Child's Play International
  How your Body Works, Usborne
  Incredible Cross-Sections by Stephen Biesty, Dorling Kindersley
  Keeping Clean: A Very Peculiar History by Daisy Kerr, Watts Books
  Knights, Kings and Conquerers by Geraldine McCaughrean, Orion Children's Books
  Pictures of Home by Colin Thompson, Julia MacRae
  War Boy: A Country Childhood by Michael Foreman, Puffin
  The Usborne Encyclopedia of World Religions by Kirsten Rogers and Clare Hickman, Usborne

- TEN AUDIO TAPES
  The Demon Headmaster by Gillian Cross, BBC Audio
  Farm Boy by Michael Morpurgo, Collins
  George Speaks by Dick King-Smith, Chivers Calvacade
  It's Not Fair! by Bel Mooney, BBC Audio
  The Owl Tree by Jenny Nimmo, BBC Audio
  The Speckled Panic by Hazel Townson, Chivers Cavalcade
  Tom and the Tree House by Joan Lingard, BBC Audio
  Twin Trouble by Jacqueline Wilson, BBC Audio
  Viking at School by Jeremy Strong, Chivers Cavalcade
  The Worst Witch by Jill Murphy, BBC Audio

- TEN CHARACTER TOYS
  Can't you Sleep, Little Bear? Walker Books
  Elmer. Rainbow Designs
  Farmer Duck. Chatterbox/Edduplush
  Kipper. Hodder Children's Books
  No Matter What Toy Set. Bloomsbury
  Owl Babies Finger Puppets. Perupets
  The Snowman. Rainbow Designs
  There was an Old Lady. Child's Play International
  The Very Busy Spider. G.P. Putnam
  The Very Hungry Caterpillar. Puffin

Presenting Stories to Children

Storytelling and reading aloud to children open new and exciting worlds and help them make sense of their own experiences and feelings and those of others. They are powerful learning experiences which not only reveal the rhythms, richness and variety of language, but also help children learn how to respond to narrative: to remember events, empathise with the characters, express their views, predict what might happen, and appreciate humour and suspense. Through storytelling and reading aloud we broaden children's experience of the spoken word, expand their appreciation of literature, help them understand how stories work and offer good models for their own storytelling and story and poetry writing. We are able to develop children's understanding of significant themes, events and characters; help them locate and express ideas, experiences and opinions; help them infer, deduce and explain their views; and assist them in developing confidence and enthusiasm in speaking and concentration in listening. Through their exposure to good-quality stories and poems, where the text is lifted from the page by a skilful reader, children also come to appreciate the importance of timing, expression, accent, tone of voice and body language.

Create the right environment, with the group of listeners sitting comfortably around you in a half circle. Allow time and space for the children to enjoy and respond to the reading.

Deliver the text clearly and slowly in a voice that is a little louder than normal conversation. Raise and lower the voice to gain effect. Avoid reading to the front row only and make frequent eye-contact with the children.

Talk to the children about the story structure: the introduction to the story, the setting of the scene, the development of the theme, the building up of characters and the conclusion.

Talk to the children about stylistic features: significant phrases, interesting details, choice of certain words, use of description and dialogue, repetition, sentence structure and figures of speech.

Demonstrate how – by using body language, gesture, pacing, intonation, pauses, expression, timing, tone of voice and accent – an atmosphere can be created and sustained.

Invite the Schools Library Service to mount a display of popular books, recommend stories and storytellers and help with reading sessions.

The Story Summary Sheet (see page 111) is useful to access the children's understanding and reinforce the work that has been undertaken in the "shared reading" sessions on plot and story structure. Clearly such a sheet would not be used on every occasion that a child reads a book. Were that the case, the children would soon be turned off reading.

Story Summary Sheet

Name of reader: ....

Title of the story: ....

Author of the story: ....

Date read: ....

The story begins when:

The first thing that happens is:

After that:

And then:

The story ends when:

Personal comment:

The Story Record

Some people find it useful to keep a record of what they have read, with brief notes about the book for future reference. A simple example that is easy to complete is shown below.

Story record

Title: **The Hodgeheg**

Author: **Dick King-Smith**

Author information:
Formerly farmer, teacher, freelance writer. Writes original, unsentimental, entertaining stories which appeal to all children.

Genre:
Amusing animal adventure story.

Plot:
The hedgehogs at Number 5A dream of reaching the park. Max sets out to solve the problem of how to get them across the busy main road.

Language:
Very accessible, lively, sometimes poetic.

Related texts:
Ace, Daggie Dogfoot, Dodos are Forever, The Fox Busters, Friends and Brothers, George Speaks, Harry's Mad, Magnus Powermouse, Martin's Mice, Noah's Brother, Paddy's Pot of Gold, The Queen's Nose, Saddlebottom, The Sheep-Pig, Sophie's Snail, Chewing the Cud.

Age range: **6-10 years**

Prompt Sheet for Guided Reading

The "guided reading" session gives you the opportunity of spending some time with each group talking about the text, listening to the children read and helping them with particular difficulties they might encounter. Guided reading is not just reading in unison round the group or silent individual reading or an opportunity for the teacher merely to "hear" readers. It is a time when children deepen and widen their understanding of the text, learn how to use aspects of language, engage in reading strategies such as prediction and self-correction, and learn the skills and strategies to read increasingly difficult material. To keep them on task the teacher might, on occasion, give each group a series of prompts. Below are some questions that may be useful during a "guided reading" session.

- Title of the story
  - What does the title make you think the story will be about?

- Author of the story
  - Have you read any other stories by this author?
  - What are the themes they usually write about?
  - Is this story different?

- Introduction
  - Read the first few paragraphs.
  - Does the opening begin with: scene setting, character description, dialogue or does it take the reader straight into the action?
  - Does it begin in another way?

- Characters
  - Identify the main characters in this story.
  - What are they like?
  - What are the most important events that happen to the characters?
  - What are the main difficulties the characters have to overcome?

- Development
  - How does the writer keep the reader's interest?
  - Did you think the story would continue in the way it did?

- Conclusion
  - Did you expect the story to end as it did?
  - Did the opening of the story prepare you for the ending?

- Language
  - Are there any descriptions, phrases or words which stood out?
  - Are there any parts of the story that you could not understand?

- Personal comment
  - What is your opinion of this story?
  - Would you like to read another story by this author?

Writing a Book Review

Children might be encouraged to write a review of a book they have read. This should be an infrequent activity. Books should be sources of pleasure and information and there is nothing more likely to discourage a young person from picking up a book than having to write a book review after every story they have read.

Children need guidance in writing a review. You might break the group up into smaller units to read a number of reviews of popular books. The children might be asked to highlight all the positive comments in one colour and all the negative ones in another. This gives the young reviewers an armoury of words to use. Certain words and phrases will appear with regularity. You may like to display the following words for the children.

In the well-written book

popular ◆ humorous ◆ strong sense of period ◆ enthralling artwork
delightful ◆ favourite ◆ sharply observed ◆ vivid descriptions
inspiring ◆ best-selling ◆ lively text ◆ detailed illustrations
absorbing ◆ wacky ◆ clear, concise style ◆ breathtaking photographs
atmospheric ◆ intriguing ◆ unputdownable ◆ wealth of information
irresistible ◆ coherent ◆ rounded characters ◆ fascinating account
entertaining ◆ amusing ◆ vibrant language ◆ dramatic pictures
exciting ◆ stimulating ◆ unforgettable ◆ strong characterisation
charming ◆ moving ◆ powerful ◆ spine-tingling

In the poorly written book

dull ◆ wearisome ◆ predictable ◆ tedious ◆ lacklustre
tiresome ◆ ponderous ◆ uninteresting ◆ contains clichés ◆ patronising
inaccurate ◆ pedestrian ◆ prosaic ◆ lifeless ◆ monotonous ◆ dreary

Children might then be asked to consider the books they have read and write a short review in the following format.

● Paragraph 1: details of the title, author and publisher and any general information that might be of interest.

● Paragraph 2: something about the story to give the reader a feel for the book and what it is about, but not giving too much away.

● Paragraph 3: a personal view and whether it is to be recommended or not.

Two Book Reviews

The National Literacy Strategy Framework states that frequent opportunities should be given for pupils to hear, read and discuss different kinds of text and to think about the content, structure, conventions and language used. The discussion of appropriate texts which offer children models for their own writing is at the heart of the Literacy Hour. Below are two book reviews, one good, the other not so good, both written by 10-year-olds. Discussion of them might help children understand how a successful book review functions.

Hurricane Summer by Robert Swindells

Hurricane Summer is quite simply the best book I have read. I knew I was in for a cracking story when I saw the author – Robert Swindells – because I have read two other books of his (the chilling *Room 13* and the gripping *Ice Palace*). I had enjoyed the fast-moving plots and realistic characters so I had an idea that this book would be a good read. I wasn't disappointed.

This short novel (less than seventy pages) is set at the time of World War Two. Young Jim, aged 10, has a fantastic new "friend", Cocky, a fighter pilot, who comes to lodge with him and his mum. Cocky is everything Jim would like to be: handsome, clever, funny and really brave. Jim's dad had been killed in the War and when Cocky comes into his life it's like having a new and exciting father. At school he describes the exciting exploits of Cocky (all made up, of course):

> Flying alone on a dawn patrol, Cocky spotted a formation of 110s. There were nine of them, but he didn't hesitate. Putting his Hurricane into a shallow dive, he got their leader in his sights and blasted him out of the sky with a burst from his eight Brownings.

Then into Jim's life comes Clive Simcox, the school bully, and Jim has some difficult decisions to make. *Hurricane Summer* is an extraordinary book. The plot races along (I read it in one reading) and it is full of wonderfully drawn characters and lively dialogue. Be prepared to laugh (there are some very amusing moments) and also to cry, because there are some very sad parts. This is a book all children should read.

Bill's New Frock by Anne Fine

Bill's New Frock is by Anne Fine. One Monday morning Bill woke up and found he was a girl. When he went to school nobody knew him in his pink dress. When he wanted to play football all the boys said, "Not a little girl," and they wouldn't let him play. Bill got really sad and at lunchtime it began to rain and he just sat by himself with a comic. Then he got mad and ended up in a fight. Everything worked out because Bill went home and the next day when he woke up he was back to normal.

The Road to Reading: A Guide for Parents

The most important thing parents can do for their children is to read with them. So many children today are just sitting in front of the television and we are becoming very poor at sharing experiences between the generations. But if you have a child on your knee with a book you are sharing it. You have the close physical contact and the child can start to talk to you. We talk about inter-activity on computers, but there's more interaction in reading a book.

Jostein Gaarder (author of *Sophie's World* and *Hello? Is Anybody There?*)

As parents you are your child's first teachers and your encouragement and support will assist their progress and development.

Sharing a story book is a valuable means of fostering a love of reading and an enthusiasm for books.

Like walking, talking and playing, reading needs a great deal of time to perfect. Just as you encourage your child to walk and talk by your support, enthusiasm and delight at simple successes, you could give encouragement along the road to reading success by adopting the same attitude.

It is important that books are seen as sources of great pleasure and an interested and sensitive adult can make reading one of life's most rewarding experiences for a young child. The physical closeness, the sense of warmth and security and your ability to lift the story from the page through reading aloud will make the child come to associate reading with enjoyment.

Reading together strengthens understanding between adult and child and develops a feeling of security and an atmosphere of confidence. It also takes away the fear of failing to read.

Your patience will be rewarded by their love of books and delight in sharing a good story.

The opportunity to share a good book with your child will arise on many occasions during the day. All children respond to a bedtime story.

Remind your child to take a book along on a visit to a doctor's surgery, the dentist or to visit relatives. That will help pass spare moments and pacify an anxious child.

You will help your child to learn to read if you encourage them to learn to value books. Help with this by looking at pictures and reading the story together. Allow your child to handle books, choose them and talk about the picture and the language use.

Books come in different shapes and sizes, with a variety of illustrations and line drawings. Some have a special feature like a hole through the middle of the page, lift-up flaps, or boxes to open to capture a child's interest and feed their curiosity.

Books like ...

The Animal Orchestra by Nick Sharratt, Walker Books

Cheese and Tomato Spider by Nick Sharratt, Scholastic Children's Books/Hippo

Haunted House by Jan Pieńkowski, Walker Books

There were Ten in a Bed by Pam Andrews, Child's Play International

The Very Hungry Caterpillar by Eric Carle, Puffin

Children need nursery rhymes, folk tales and fairy stories which introduce them to the rhythms and rhymes of the language and which are part of our literary heritage.

> **Books like ...**
> *A Twist in the Tale*, edited by Mary Hoffman, illustrated by Jan Ormerod, Frances Lincoln
> *Fairy Tales*, retold by Berlie Doherty, illustrated by Jane Ray, Walker Books
>
> *Fairy Tales and Fantastic Stories* by Terry Jones, Pavilion
> *The Hefty Fairy* by Nicholas Allan, Red Fox
> *The Town Mouse and the Country Mouse* by Helen Craig, Walker Books

In addition young children need to come across stories from other cultures and about people of other lands.

> **Books like ...**
> *A Bag of Moonshine* by Alan Garner, HarperCollins
> *Lost in Africa* by Nick Warburton, Walker Books
> *100 World Myths and Legends* by Geraldine McCaughrean, Dolphin
>
> *Rainforest* by Helen Cowcher, Milet Ltd
> *Wee Willie Winkie*, edited by Iona Opie, illustrated by Rosemary Wells, Walker Books

When you have chosen your books together, talk about the cover, the shape and size, and the title to raise interest and expectation.

You might sit your child on your knee to read the story. Physical closeness will help concentration and create the happy, relaxed atmosphere which is necessary.

You might look at the pictures, talk about them and relate them to the story. Sharing a book is not a test and getting impatient or angry with a child who does not seem interested will not help. You need to stimulate their interest.

Expect and encourage your child to pick out from the story aspects of interest.

Each week new and exciting children's books appear on the market about different people, places and subjects, written in a range of styles and with a variety of illustration and print.

> **Books like ...**
> *Angelina Ballerina* by Katherine Holabird, illustrated by Helen Craig, Puffin
> *Lost in the Snow* by Ian Beck, Scholastic Children's Books
>
> *Pumpkin Soup* by Helen Cooper, Doubleday/ Picture Corgi
> *Twiddling Your Thumbs* by Wendy Cope, Faber
> *Willy the Dreamer* by Anthony Browne, Walker Books

Your local public library will have a wide range of books suitable for the pre-school child as well as for the developing reader. Parents can also ask the librarian for advice about appropriate books for children.

When your child starts school your interest in their reading is still important. Do continue to read together, discuss books and visit the bookshop and library. Teachers want all children to enjoy reading and will provide opportunities for your child to learn through a variety of books, activities and experiences, but your interest and involvement will make an enormous contribution to success.

Presenting Poetry to Children

Poetry is accorded an important place in the National Curriculum and in the National Literacy Strategy Framework. We are charged with introducing a broad range of verse to children, encouraging them to enjoy and appreciate the rhymes and rhythms of the language and learn the skills to write good-quality poems themselves. Children are entitled, from the very earliest age, to hear and study a range of material which is rich and varied: funny, exciting, spooky, vigorous, fresh, playful, reflective verse; poems of intensity and excitement, in which the language is crisp, clear and forceful; and rhymes full of pleasures and surprises. You might heighten children's awareness of poetry by using a range of strategies. These could include the following.

1. Read a wide selection of poems to children over the year. For example, you might start the day with a poem – not to be discussed or analysed, just to be enjoyed. There does not always have to be follow-on work. Simply reading poetry to children "attunes their ear" with the richest kind of language.

2. Compile a list of poems suitable for different age groups and make a collection of poetry posters and cards.

3. Invite poets into school to work with the children and share their experiences of the process of writing: where ideas come from, the research they have to undertake, and how they draft and revise, proof read and submit for publication. Listening to poets like Mike Gowar, Peter Dixon, Adrian Mitchell, Pie Corbett, Brian Moses, Roger McGough and Berlie Doherty reading and interpreting their own work will fascinate and inspire children. The poet's visit might be arranged as part of a book week or literature festival and the local Arts Group, a publisher or the Poetry Society (22 Betterton Street, London WC2H 9BX) will be able to advise and may be able to help with funding. *The Address Book* is an ideal starting point from which to contact such authors.

4. Display a wide selection of material and ask the children to browse. Then, from an anthology, select just one short verse – perhaps a limerick or a haiku. Ask each child to copy out the selected poem and decorate it, commit it to memory and then recite it to the others in the class. A collection of these short poems could be put together into a poetry booklet or form part of a colourful display.

5. Mount displays of poetry anthologies, book jackets and posters in school corridors and classrooms. Publishers will often provide material.

6. Organise an evening for teachers, parents, governors and children when a speaker such as an author, adviser or member of the Schools Library Service talks about the importance of poetry. As part of the event the children could be asked to read or perform a selection of poems (including their own) accompanied by music and mime. This could include a dramatic reading or a group choral presentation.

7. Spend a little time each week reading and discussing a longer, more demanding poem. When studying a poem in the Literacy Hour do so sensitively. Appreciation comes before analysis.

8. Enlarge short poems and hang them from the ceilings or decorate classrooms, libraries and corridors with them. The range of colourful and varied pictorial charts and poetry posters produced by PCET Publishing, 27 Kirchen Road, London W13 0UD, will brighten up any classroom or corridor and raise the profile of poetry in school. They can be used for shared reading activities in the Literacy Hour.

9. If you have a computer, leave it on with a poem screen saver.

10. Integrate poetry into the topic work you undertake. The Poetry Society produces an excellent range of poetry packs which contain posters, books and support materials.

The Benefits of an Author Visit

Authors working with children can contribute at many levels to pupil learning. I have visited and worked in many schools – with Bernard Ashley, Helen Cowcher, Peter Dixon, Adèle Geras, Debi Gliori, Chris Powling, Michael Rosen, Hazel Townson and many more authors – and have seen at first hand the impact they have on young people. They do all of the following.

- *Give an insight into the world of the author*
  Children love to meet the creators of the books they read. They are fascinated to hear how and why they became authors, where their ideas come from, the training they undertook, where they work, when they started writing, and how long it took to write or illustrate a book. They gain insight into the craft of writing and illustrating and come to appreciate the commitment and dedication of authors.

- *Offer role models*
  Visiting authors provide role models and opportunities for children to develop positive relationships with adults other than their teachers.

- *Explore the artistic process*
  Working with a professional author helps children to understand more about the process of writing and illustrating. They learn that authors find inspiration in a variety of sources: for example people they meet, places they have visited, their own and other cultures, and the work of other authors. They learn about the importance of research, planning, deciding on the audience, the purpose and the form of the writing or the style of illustration. They learn that the professional author experiments with different ideas, just as they are encouraged to experiment by their teachers; that authors too draft and rework, edit and proof read. You can encourage children to redraft their work but it is often regarded as a chore and may become little more than making a fair copy. Working with a writer demonstrates that the professional author does not produce at their first attempt a piece of work that is ready to be published.

- *Encourage the sharing of work*
  Authors can provide opportunities for children to share their work with a wider audience than the teacher. Children can produce a booklet, create a web site, mount a display and present the work to parents.

- *Foster enthusiasm*

  A writer or artist working in school, and displaying an open and uninhibited enthusiasm for their craft, can win over a whole hall full of adolescents despite strong peer pressure to appear uninterested.

- *Develop confidence*

  Some pupils lack confidence in sharing their work with adults. Sometimes an author can act as a catalyst, offering children the opportunity for showing and discussing their work and asking for advice.

Writing to an Author

The writing process involves establishing a purpose and an audience and deciding on what form the writing will take. What is it for? Who is it for? What kind of writing is it to be? Then follows planning, drafting, revising and editing.

Of all the forms of writing, it is perhaps the letter that demonstrates this process best to children. There is a clear reason for writing, a perceived audience and a set format with heading, salutation, content and signature. Children need to plan the letter, draft it, make revisions and seek help from you to check it through for omissions and errors. Then, in a clear, legible hand, they produce the final effort.

Quite apart from learning about the writing process, there are many other benefits to be gained when children write to authors and illustrators. The exercise demonstrates that writers and artists are real people, it demystifies writing and illustrating, deepens the reader's understanding of a particular author's or illustrator's work, and encourages reading and research.

Here are a few pointers for would-be letter writers.

1. Letters should emerge from a lesson in the natural context of reading and studying literature and art. They should not form part of a letter-writing or hand-writing exercise. Encourage children to write individual letters rather than copy a set letter from the board with suggested questions.

2. Make certain the letter writer has read the author's book.

3. Allow the children to write to the author of their choice.

4. Discuss appropriate questions with the children.

5. Encourage the children to be honest, original, sincere, thoughtful and spontaneous in their letters; to show genuine curiosity; to relate some of their own experiences; to raise interesting questions; and to say how the story, poem or illustration made them feel. Remember to read the letters before they are sent out.

6. Limit the number of letters to a particular author; they are busy people, often without secretarial help, and cannot reply individually to a large batch of letters. It is often a good idea to write one letter from the whole class. If a batch of letters is sent, expect a single response.

7. Limit the number of questions. Some questions, for example about an author's life and background, can be answered by reading the information on a book jacket.

8. Include a stamped addressed A4 envelope.

9. Write a covering letter – a personal note to introduce the children.

10. Letters are sometimes forwarded to authors by publishers several weeks after the initial posting, so do not set unrealistic goals for a reply.

11. Do not send long manuscripts from aspiring writers. If stories, poems and illustrations are included, do not expect the author to write a detailed critique.

12. Remember that Poetry Day, Reading Week and other national events are busy times for authors.

13. Share the letters received from authors with the class and perhaps with a wider audience. You could mount a display, or compile a small collection in booklet form.

Arranging a Visit from an Author

Many children's authors are willing to work in schools, talking to children and teachers about the writing process or the creation of their illustrations. Some run workshop-based activities, contribute to in-service courses and conferences and attend book weeks and festivals. Regional Arts Boards and Local Education Authorities may be able to help with funding.

It is essential that any visit arranged with an author is scrupulously planned. Below are the top twenty tips.

1. Choose your author with care.
2. Study their work.
3. Make initial approaches through the publisher by letter, including a stamped addressed envelope.
4. Suggest dates and times.
5. Once the arrangements have been made, confirm them by letter.
6. Give appropriate information about the school and the pupils.
7. Outline briefly what you hope to gain from the visit.
8. Do not expect an author to attend meetings before or after the visit unless you can offer payment.
9. Agree the fee and any additional expenses.
10. Ask the publisher for any suitable posters, postcards, book jackets and publicity material.
11. Agree on a programme for the day, including the length of sessions, whom the author will be working with, the group sizes and the focus of the visit.
12. Provide additional information such as a map to the school, arrangements for lunch and breaks.
13. Notify the local press.
14. Study the author's work with the children prior to the visit.
15. Have copies of the author's work available during the visit.

16. Give the children the opportunity of buying the author's work.
17. Ensure that you supervise the children during the workshop.
18. Inform the local bookshop and library of the author's visit.
19. Ensure that everyone in the school, including the school secretary, is expecting the author.
20. Most authors are self-employed, so payment should be prompt.

2. Essential Details

Addresses of Children's Literature Organisations

Centre for Language in Primary Education
Webber Street
London
SE1 8QW
Tel: 020 7401 3382/3
Fax: 020 7928 4624
www.clpe.co.uk

National Association for the Teaching of English (NATE)
50 Broadfield Road
Sheffield
S8 0XJ
Tel: 0114 255 5419
Fax: 0114 255 5296
nate.hq@btconnect.com

The National Literacy Trust
Swire House
59 Buckingham Gate
London
SW1E 6AJ
Tel: 020 7828 2435
Fax: 020 7931 9986
Contact@literacytrust.org.uk
www.literacytrust.org.uk
see also www.rif.org.uk

Reading and Language Information Centre
University of Reading
Bulmershe Court
Earley, Reading
Berkshire RG6 1HY
Tel: 0118 931 8820
Fax: 0118 931 6801
reading-centre@reading.ac.uk
www.ralic.reading.ac.uk

School Library Association
Unit 2, Lotmead Business Village
Lotmead Farm
Wanborough
Swindon SN4 0UY
Tel: 01793 791 787
Fax: 01793 791 786
info@SLA.org.uk

United Kingdom Reading Association (UKRA)
Unit 6, First Floor
The Maltings, Green Drift
Royston
Hertfordshire SG8 5DB
Tel: 01763 241 188
Fax: 01763 243 785
admin@ukra.org
www.ukra.org

Addresses of Regional Arts Boards

Arts Council of England
14 Great Peter Street
London
SW1P 3NQ
Tel: 020 7333 0100
Fax: 020 7973 6590
Minicom: 020 7973 6564
www.artscouncil.org.uk

Arts Council of Wales
Museum Place
Cardiff
CF10 3NX
Tel: 02920 376 500
Fax: 02920 221 447
Minicom: 02920 390 027
information@ccc-acw.org.uk
www.ccc-acw.org.uk

Scottish Arts Council
12 Manor Place
Edinburgh EH3 7DD
Tel: 0131 226 6051
Fax: 0131 225 9833
Email:
administrator@scottisharts.org.uk
www.sac.org.uk

East England Arts
Eden House
48–49 Bateman Street
Cambridge CB2 1LR
Tel: 01223 454 400
Fax: 0870 242 1271
Minicom: 01223 306 893
info@eearts.co.uk
www.eastenglandarts.co.uk

East Midlands Arts
Mountfields House
Epinal Way
Loughborough
Leicestershire LE11 0QE
Tel: 01509 218 292
www.arts.org.uk

London Arts
2 Pear Tree Court
London EC1R 0DS
Tel: 020 7608 6100
Fax: 020 7608 4100
www.arts.org.uk

North West Arts Board
Manchester House
22 Bridge Street
Manchester M3 3AB
Tel: 0161 834 6644
Fax: 0161 834 6969
info@nwarts.co.uk
www.art.org.uk/nwab

Northern Arts
Central Square
Forth Street
Newcastle upon Tyne NE2 3PJ
Tel: (Switch & Minicom):
0191 255 8500
Fax: 0191 230 1020
info@northernarts.co.uk

South East Arts
Union House
Eridge Road
Tunbridge Wells
Kent
TN4 8HF
Tel: 01892 507 200
Fax: 01892 549 383
info@seab.co.uk
www.arts.org.uk

South West Arts
Bradninch Place
Gandy Street
Exeter
Devon
EX4 3LS
Tel: 01392 218 188
Fax: 01392 413 554
www.swa.co.uk

Southern Arts
13 St Clement Street
Winchester
Hampshire
SO23 9DQ
Tel: 01962 855 099
Fax: 0870 242 1257
info@southernarts.co.uk
www.arts.org.uk/sa

West Midlands Arts
82 Granville Street
Birmingham
B1 2LH
Tel: 0121 631 3121
Fax: 0121 643 7239
Minicom/Textphone: 0121 643 2815
info@west-midlands-arts.co.uk
www.west-midlands.arts.org.uk

Yorkshire Arts
21 Bond Street
Dewsbury
West Yorkshire
WF13 1AX
Tel: 01924 455 555
Fax: 01924 466 522

Useful Journals

Books for Keeps
6 Brightfield Road
Lee
London
SE12 8QF
Tel: 020 8852 4953
Fax: 020 8318 7580
booksforkeeps@btinternet.com

Children's Book News
Young Booktrust
Book House
45 East Hill
London
SW18 2QZ

Child Education, Junior Education and Nursery Education
Subscription Department
Scholastic Ltd
Westfield Road
Southam
Leamington Spa
Warwickshire
CV47 0RA

Education Life Magazine
30a McDonald Street
Birmingham
B5 6TG
Tel: 0121 666 7053/4
Fax: 0121 622 7255

English 4–11
City of Salford Education Centre
London Street
Salford
M6 6QT
Tel: 0161 743 4287
Fax: 0161 743 4249

Guardian Education Supplement
119 Farrington Road
London
EC1R 3ER

Literacy & Learning
Questions Publishing
Frederick Street
Hockley
Birmingham
B1 3HH
Tel: 0121 212 0939
Fax: 0121 212 0959

Literacy Today
The National Literacy Trust
Swine House
59 Buckingham Gate
London
SW1E 6AJ
Tel: 020 7828 2435
Fax: 020 7931 9986

Signal
The Thimble Press
Lockwood Station Road
South Woodchester
Stroud
Gloucestershire GL5 5EQ
Tel: 01453 755 566/872 208
Fax: 01453 878 599

The Times Education Supplement/Primary Magazine
Admiral House
66–68 East Smithfield
London
E1W 9XY
Tel: 0207 782 3000
Fax: 0207 782 3333

Selected Children's Book Awards

The following list of children's books awards may help you to choose books for your children to read, and also authors to invite to your school.

Caldecott Medal

This annual award is presented for the outstanding American picture book of that year. It is named after the English illustrator Randolph Caldecott. It is announced each January/February.

Carnegie Medal

This award is announced in July and is given for an outstanding book for children published during the preceding year.

Children's Book Award

There are three categories of this award: picture, short novel and longer novel. From each of these categories an overall winner is chosen. The winners are announced in June for the previous year.

Guardian Children's Fiction Award

The winner of this award is announced each September. It is given to a British or Commonwealth author who, during the preceding year, is adjudged to have produced an outstanding work of fiction (excluding picture books).

Kate Greenaway Medal

This award, announced every July, is given to the artist who has produced the most outstanding work in the illustration of children's books in the UK during the previous year.

Newbery Medal

Announced every January/February, this award is given for the most distinguished contribution to American children's literature during the preceding year. The award commemorates the London bookseller John Newbery.

Whitbread Children's Book of the Year Award

This award, for a children's novel produced during the previous year, is announced each January. The winner has to have been resident in the UK or Eire for at least three years.

Select Bibliography

Barber, M. (1997). Transforming Standards in Literacy, in McClelland, N. (ed.) *Building a Literate Nation*. London, National Literacy Trust in collaboration with Trentham Books.

Beard, R. (1990). *Developing Reading, 3–13*. London, Hodder and Stoughton.

Bennett, J. (1982). *A Choice of Stories*. Swindon, The School Library Association.

Bettelheim, B. and Zelan, K. (1991). *On Learning to Read: The Child's Fascination with Meaning*. London, Penguin.

Clark, M. (1976) *Young Fluent Readers*. London. Heinemann Educational.

Colwell, E. (1991). *Story Telling*. Stroud, Thimble Press.

Cowley, J. *et al.* (1993). *The Story Chest: Teacher's File*. Walton-on-Thames, Thomas Nelson.

DES (1989). *English in the National Curriculum, Programme of Study for Reading at Key Stage 1*. London, HMSO.

DES (1990). *English in the National Curriculum*. London, HMSO.

DES (1990). *The Teaching and Learning of Reading in Primary Schools*. London, HMSO.

DfEE. (1998). *The National Literacy Strategy: The Management of Literacy at School Level*. London, DfEE Press.

DfEE. (1998). *National Year of Reading: Getting Ready*. London, DfEE Press.

Graham, J. and Plackett, E. (1987). *Developing Readers*. Swindon, The School Library Association.

Jones, A. and Buttrey, J. (1970). *Children and Stories*. Oxford, Blackwell.

Marum, E. (ed.) (1995). *Towards 2000: The Future of Childhood, Literacy and Schooling*. London, The Falmer Press.

Meek, M. (1984). *Learning to Read*. London. The Bodley Head.

Meek, M. *et al.* (1977). *The Cool Web: The Pattern of Children's Reading*. London, The Bodley Head.

Meek, M., Warlow, A. and Barton, G. (eds.) (1988). *How Texts Teach What Readers Learn*. Stroud, Thimble Press.

Neate, B. (ed.) (1996). *Literacy Saves Lives*. Shepreth, The United Kingdom Reading Association Press.

O'Connor, M. (1990). *How to Help your Child through School*. London, Harrap.

Phinn, G. (1986). Fiction in the Classroom, in Blatchford, R. (ed.) *The English Teacher's Handbook*. London, Hutchinson.

Phinn, G. (1987). No Language to Speak of? Children Talking and Writing, in Booth, T. *et al.* (eds.) *Preventing Difficulties in Learning: Curricula for All*. Oxford, Basil Blackwell in association with the Open University Press.

Phinn, G. (1992). Choosing Books for Young Readers: Habituated to the Vast, in Harrison, C. and Coles, M. (eds.) *The Reading for Real Handbook*. London, Routledge.

Phinn, G. (1993). *The Vital Resource: Poetry in the Primary School.* Huddersfield, Woodfield and Stanley Ltd.

Phinn, G. (1995). *Touches of Beauty: Teaching Poetry in the Primary School.* Doncaster, Roselea Publications.

Phinn, G. (2000). *Young Readers and their Books.* London, David Fulton Publishers.

Tucker, N. (1990). *The Child and the Book: A Psychological and Literary Exploration.* Cambridge, Cambridge University Press.

Waterland, L. (ed.) (1988). *Read with Me: An Apprenticeship Approach to Reading.* Stroud, Thimble Press.

Permissions in order of appearance of copyright material

Illustration from *Beyond the Deepwoods* © 1998 Chris Riddell. Text © 1998 Paul Stewart. Published by Doubleday. Reproduced by permission of The Random House Group Ltd.

'Wizard's Advice to Baby Dragon' Text © 2001 Philip Ridley. Reproduced by permission of the author.

Illustration from *Harold the Hairiest Man* © 1997 Tony Ross. Text © 1997 Laurence Anholt. Reproduced by permission of the publisher, Orchard Books, a division of The Watts Publishing Group Ltd.

Illustration from *Buzz Buzz Bumble Jelly* © 2000 Nick Sharratt. Reproduced by permission of the publisher, Scholastic Children's Book, Scholastic Ltd.

Illustration from *Lulu and the Flying Babies* © 1988 Posy Simmonds. Published by Jonathan Cape. Reproduced by permission of The Random House Group Ltd.

Extract from *Beyond the Deepwoods* Text © 1998 Paul Stewart. Illustrations ©1998 Chris Riddell. Published by Doubleday. Reproduced by permission of The Random House Group Ltd.

Extract from *My Mum's Going to Explode!* Text © 2001 Jeremy Strong. Illustrations © 2001 Nick Sharratt. Reproduced by permission of David Higham Associates.

Extract from *The Leap Text* © 2000 Jonathan Stroud. Published by Bodley Head/ Red Fox. Reproduced by permission of The Random House Group Ltd.

Extract from *Stone Cold* Text © 1995 Robert Swindells. Published by Puffin. Reproduced by permission of Penguin Books Ltd.

Extract from *The Dragon Who Ate Our School* Text © 1996 Nick Toczek. Illustrations © 1996 Sally Townsend. Reproduced by permission of the publisher, Macmillan Publishers Ltd.

Extract from *The Intruder* Text © 2001 John Rowe Townsend. Reproduced by permission of the publisher, Oxford University Press.

Extract from 'Hypnotic Fit' written for *Punch* Text © 1958 Hazel Townson. Reproduced by permission of Punch Ltd.

Extract from *Here Come the Heebie-Jeebies and Other Scary Poems* Text © Kaye Umansky. Published by Hodder/Wayland. Reproduced by permission of the author.

Extract from *Fruit and Nutcase* Text © 2002 Jean Ure. Reproduced by permission of the publisher, HarperCollins Publishers Ltd.

Extract from *Farmer Duck* Text © 1991 Martin Waddell. Illustrations © 1991 Helen Oxenbury. Reproduced by permission of the publisher, Walker Books Ltd, London.

Extract from *The Strange Change of Flora Young* Text © 2001 Nick Warburton. Reproduced by permission of the publisher, Walker Books Ltd, London.

Illustration and extract from *The Big Book of Nonsense* © 2001 Colin West. Published by Hutchinson. Reproduced by permission of The Random House Group Ltd.

Illustration from *Mary* © 2002 Brian Wildsmith. Reproduced by permission of the publisher, Oxford University Press.

Extract from *Double Act* Text © 1996 Jacqueline Wilson. Illustrations © 1996 Nick Sharratt and Sue Heap. Published by Corgi Yearling. Reprinted by permission of The Random House Group Ltd.

Extract from *Talking Turkeys* Text © 1995 Benjamin Zephaniah. Published by Puffin. Reproduced by permission of Penguin Books Ltd.

Every effort has been made to obtain permission for the inclusion in this book of quoted material. Apologies are offered to anyone whom it has not been possible to contact.